Praise for *Ways and Means for Managing Up*

"A terrific book by one of the masters of truth-telling in the American military—wise, forceful, and a must-read for anyone who has a boss. Bill Smullen helped many an officer—and reporter (including this one)—navigate the treacherous landscape of war, peace, security policy, and controversy. My hat is off to him, and so will yours when you read what he has learned over the decades."

Bob Woodward, Associate Editor,
The Washington Post, and author of 17 books

"Bill Smullen's unique experience as a member of the U.S. Army and later chief of staff for former Chairman of the Joint Chiefs of Staff and Secretary of State Colin Powell gives him some great lessons to pass on. I especially appreciate the manner in which he incorporates the value of 'team play' into *Ways and Means for Managing Up*. I highly recommend it."

Jim Boeheim, Syracuse University's
Hall of Fame Head Basketball Coach

"Colonel William Smullen has worked in senior management positions for some of the most important institutions in the world, most notably the U.S. military and the U.S. State Department. Colonel Smullen has also worked for some of the smartest and most demanding bosses in modern American history, most notably General Colin Powell for many years. In his book *Ways and Means for Managing Up*, Smullen distills his half century of experience as both a manager and a subordinate to craft an invaluable guide for how to succeed inside any organization. It is a guide that is both tremendously wise and, in some places, laugh-out-loud funny."

Peter Bergen, CNN's National Security Analyst,
and author of *Manhunt: The Ten-Year Search for
Bin Laden from 9/11 to Abbottabad*

To Lauryn,

WAYS AND
MEANS FOR
MANAGING UP

May success be with
you wherever you go.
Good luck!

Bill Smullen

WAYS AND MEANS FOR MANAGING UP

50 STRATEGIES FOR HELPING YOU AND YOUR BOSS SUCCEED

F. WILLIAM SMULLEN

New York   Chicago   San Francisco   Athens   London   Madrid
Mexico City   Milan   New Delhi   Singapore   Sydney   Toronto

1 2 3 4 5 6 7 8 9 0   QFR/QFR   1 2 0 9 8 7 6 5 4

ISBN   978-0-07-182524-5
MHID   0-07-182524-X

e-ISBN 978-0-07-182652-5
e-MHID   0-07-182652-1

McGraw-Hill Education books are available at special quantity discounts to use as premiums and sales promotions or for use in corporate training programs. To contact a representative, please visit the Contact Us pages at www.mhprofessional.com.

To my late parents, Fred and Helen

Mentors for Life

Contents

Preface

Sir Winston Churchill has inspired generations with his words. He could have been talking about my inspiration to write this book for those who might benefit from it when he said, "We make a living by what we get, but we make a life by what we give."

Serving others by what you do and how you do it is a meaningful thing. It's priceless when it's done for your boss, who counts on those around him or her to do or be many of the things reflected here.

If you find a way to serve your boss better by reading this book, I hope the power of the example you set will take you down a new and brighter path in your chosen profession. Travel it well and enjoy the journey.

Bill Smullen
April 2014

Introduction

We slipped into the backseat of his limo, heading off to another event in the nation's capital. That happened often for General Colin Powell as Joint Chiefs chairman and for me as his assistant.

In the 10-minute ride that lay before us, I knew I could grab Powell's undivided attention. I intended to tell him I'd received an offer of another job for another boss, a pretty big one at that: a former president of the United States.

He nodded as I told him I'd been asked to be the PR guy for Ronald Reagan. When I finished, my proud moment was met at first with silence.

Then he turned his head and looked me in the eye. "Congratulations," he said. "But don't become intoxicated with the offer of power."

He was right, and I knew it. Fortunately, I had declined the offer, but I felt I owed it to him to tell him that it had come from President Reagan, a man for whom he had worked as his national security advisor years earlier. I wished for no surprises.

I knew I had the boss I wanted. I also felt I wanted to serve him longer and even better. One doesn't have to be of high rank or position to want to do that.

Whether you are starting out in professional life or have been part of it for some time, you have a boss and a responsibility to manage him or her like the other resources for which you're responsible.

As you advance hierarchically closer to the person to whom you are responsible, the challenges grow stronger, as does the satisfaction if you do the job well. It helps to have strategic vision, core values, and obtainable objectives as you do so. Managing yourself and those to whom you answer sets a powerful personal example and provides for functional excellence within an organization. It doesn't hurt when such efforts are rewarded with job satisfaction, advancement within the organization, and even a promotion and a raise. Helping your boss helps you.

This is a book for those who accept responsibility for taking care of the boss. It is a guide to the ways and means to help manage that boss effectively.

My 50 years of managing and leading others have led to many experiences of how to do or not do things in ways that are either helpful or hurtful. Taking care of business by making the boss look good was something I strived for each and every day in each and every way.

Not only does it provide a strategic advantage in moving from one good job to the next, it is a value-added proposition for the organization and the people in it. Managing yourself and others well is of paramount importance in your professional life. Results like those described in this book can expand your portfolio of accomplishments and move you from a position of good to one of great.

WAYS AND MEANS FOR MANAGING UP

1

Believe in Your Boss
or Find Another

Bosses come in all shapes and sizes. They also come with a variety of temperaments and management styles. Some are easy to like; others are not even easy to be around.

As a subordinate, you may think you are stuck with the boss you have and the job you hold. I would argue there is a different way, a better way. If you're not happy with either your boss or your position, find another. However, I wouldn't recommend quitting unless you have somewhere to go or someone new to go to.

It's incumbent for each of us to ask these questions: "Do I believe in my boss?" "Can I follow my boss?" "Do I like my boss?" If the answer to all three is yes, you are in a good place and should stick with what you have been doing and are doing in your professional life.

If you believe in your boss, it's fairly easy to follow what he or she has to say or asks you to do. If you do not, it's time to find another boss.

What if you love your job and the work you do but you are not so crazy about the boss? This can be a dilemma. Moreover, it may require some action.

I had two bosses during the course of my military career with whom I simply didn't get along. It was a bad fit in both situations.

They were terrible leaders; they were horrible managers. They both appeared to have had charismatic bypasses.

I tried to make it work and was respectful toward them, but I finally chose to deal with the situation straight on. In both cases, I waited until after normal duty hours, when fellow staffers were gone. I knocked on their respective doors and asked if we could talk. I told them I was not comfortable with our relationship and asked how it might be repaired. They responded as I had expected. They mumbled something about our having to work toward improving things. I sensed they meant that I had to make some changes.

In both cases I did my share of attempting to improve things, yet nothing seemed to change. I worked hard while moving in a direction that would lead me to reassignment. In both instances, I was chosen for an even better position of responsibility and moved on to a better place professionally.

When faced with such a dilemma, you might seek a lateral transfer. There have been cases in which people have taken a step over or down or even a cut in pay to find a better way.

However, if you're one of the lucky ones and love your boss, that makes it easier to come to work every day. I've even known people who can't wait to get to work, some who brag about what they do when they get there, some who even sing the boss's praises. What a great place to be.

This may sound like a simple test, but it's worth taking. Most of us have to look in the mirror each morning to wash our faces and brush our teeth. Same thing at the end of the day.

When doing this in the morning, you can ask yourself this question: "Am I going off today to do something important?" It doesn't mean you have to save the world or change the course of Western civilization. But if the answer is yes, you are headed in the right direction.

If at the end of the day you ask the question "Did I do something of value today?" or "Did I make a difference?" and the answer is yes, you're in a good place. You may want to stay where you are.

However, in this age of upward and outward mobility most people will experience several jobs in their professional careers. Don't fear moving on if you don't enjoy your job. There probably is something better out there for everyone.

On the other hand, what if the problem is you? What if it's not so much how good a boss you have but the fact that you can't relate to that boss or any boss? You indeed may be the problem.

If you are, you need to either fix the situation or find another path in which you are the person of least resistance. If you don't, you're just a clog in the wheel of progress.

We should all have golden rules to live by, ones that will serve us well. When it comes to bosses, there's a general rule to help guide you: you don't have to love 'em, you don't even have to like 'em, but you need to remember that the boss is always the boss. That being the case, you need to work consciously with and for him or her to obtain the best possible results for you, your boss, and the organization for which you work. You won't regret it.

2

Be Forever Loyal
and Faithful to the Boss

In this day and age, it is not uncommon for people to have multiple jobs, work for multiple organizations, or have multiple bosses over time or throughout a career. Moving from one job to another is common, and it can be good for you both personally and professionally.

But with that mobility comes challenge. Getting to know the ropes, getting into a routine, and getting to transfer loyalties are responsibilities that go with a new job.

Learning a new culture isn't so difficult in most cases, nor is adapting to a new routine or even a new dress code. What is difficult in some cases is transferring loyalty from one boss to the next.

Before you take a new job or are assigned to a new position, it helps to ask, "Is this a good fit for me?" If it's all about money or title, it may not be. If you've asked yourself whether this "dream job" is truly for you, you've taken a good first step. If you don't have a choice because of the transfer of either you or your new boss to the organization, the challenge may be greater.

Either way, you need to invest yourself in the new conditions in which you find yourself. Part of that investment is being loyal and faithful to what and whom you have inherited.

Make a case with the new boss that will convincingly prove your value to him or her. Your professionalism will go a long way toward gaining the boss's confidence in you. If you impress the boss early by knowing what he or she cares most about, you will be off and running.

A lot of what you're striving for is trust. But you have to give before you can expect to gain that trust. This is the key to building a winning relationship with the leader to whom you are responsible.

That starts by getting to know him or her. Learn what the boss has set for goals and apply functional excellence to help achieve them. Learn to think like the boss so that it's a good fit. Be all you can be.

If you are in the position of high responsibility on the hierarchical ladder, you need to influence others in positive ways when there is change in their lives too. You have a responsibility to encourage their loyalty and faithfulness to the organization and the boss. You must set an example.

What if you have two or more bosses with very different personalities, different temperaments, or different management styles? You need to be accepting of those differences, and it's up to you to work with whatever demands come with them.

Like everyone, bosses have their imperfections, even their limitations. Nevertheless, they deserve respect, understanding, support, and allegiance.

Transferring loyalty and being faithful can work in reverse. If the new boss isn't convinced that you are trustworthy, loyal, and faithful, you may be the one who is under scrutiny.

This happened to me. In just a year I had built a firm and durable relationship with Admiral William J. Crowe as his special assistant. When he announced his retirement as chairman of the Joint Chiefs of Staff, I had to make a decision to move on or take a position with the new chairman, General Colin L. Powell. It wasn't my decision alone to make, for Powell knew of my friendship with and closeness to the admiral, and I sensed that he wasn't confident that I could transfer my loyalty to him.

I underwent the test he imposed. He summoned me for an interview. He asked some tough questions about what I could do for him and how I would do it. Since a new chairman can hire, fire, or bring staff with him, this was not a pro forma proposition. Fortunately, I passed and he chose to retain me as his special assistant. As it turned out, the relationship lasted for the next 13 years, during which I worked for him in several capacities.

I pledged to myself every day that I would continue to earn his trust and confidence, for he had given me his. I vowed never to let him regret hiring me. That is the two-way street that seniors and subordinates should travel together. You should view it as a partnership in which you are seen as an indispensable part of the management team.

3

Think of Your Boss
as a Brand

You see the term all the time on the business pages of the newspaper or hear it used on television to describe something or someone in trouble. It's called a brand. There are a lot of them out there. A country has a brand, the president has a brand, a corporation or an institution has a brand. So does a product.

What is a brand? It's an image, an impression, a reputation. It's not what you think you are or what you say you are. A brand is what you do, how you do it, and why.

This is an era of perception relevance. Investing in your brand is critical so that others will think well of you. If your brand, your culture, your policies, or your values are being questioned or are in jeopardy, one way to protect them is to build trust.

I like to think of it as a trust bank, like that piggy bank you had as a child and put your simple treasures in to save for the future. Focus on building trust first and restoring it second. If you have it in the bank, it is easier to repair the damage if you experience a setback. It's a lot like preventive medicine. Keep your brand healthy with good care and feeding.

It doesn't take much to tarnish a brand. It can happen to a company such as Toyota, to a product such as Tylenol, or to an individual such as Tiger Woods.

You don't have to be Tiger to have a brand. Your boss has a brand. Why? Because he or she represents something or somebody. You have a responsibility to help burnish that brand.

You want your boss to be perceived as the best he or she can be. You want your boss to be seen as someone who leads an organization well.

It's not only good for business; it's good for maintaining relationships with stakeholders. Those stakeholders include the public at large, the community in which you live and work, customers, clients, government officials, the media, and, most important, the employees.

Successful branding is about providing information and education to stakeholders about what you do, how you do it, and why. It's about promotion, but not the kind you buy. It's about earning the attention of stakeholders by being the best you can be. It's about having a dialogue with them so that they know about you and you hear what they have to say. It's about having strong relationships with each and every one of the multiple stakeholder groups to which you are responsible.

It's about unique and cutting-edge messaging that informs people *about* your boss and your organization and draws people *to* your boss and your organization. It's about preparing messages that answer the who, what, when, where, and how questions that others have about your boss and your organization. It's about having core values that you can talk about.

In this twenty-first-century world, the emergence of a new global information system has been so fast and so interlinked that everything a person or an organization does or fails to do about the brand is transparent and obvious to the stakeholders. One must stay ahead of that wave or fall victim to the current.

I have been responsible for the reputations of prominent people such as Bill Crowe and Colin Powell, the eleventh and twelfth chairmen of the Joint Chiefs of Staff. I've been responsible for the images of institutions such as the U.S. Army and organizations such as America's Promise—The Alliance for Youth.

Each one was a brand each and every day in each and every way. I would ask myself continually what were they doing, how they were doing it, and why. I did that because I knew someone else out there would ask the same questions. These are questions that you need to ask yourself continually on behalf of your boss.

If you make your boss's brand as bright as it can be, the two things you can build and maintain for the boss are reputation and credibility. The reputation is what others think of your boss, and the credibility is whether others believe in your boss. If either is lost, the boss is doomed. Your job is to never let that happen.

Managing a brand requires a lifetime of work. Brands are fragile, even the best of them. The success of any brand is not an entitlement; it has to be earned every day. It is often your most valuable organizational or individual asset, one worth building and burnishing.

4

Know More Than Is Expected

Much like preparing for a final exam in high school or a comprehensive exam in college, you should go into any test knowing more than will be asked of you. It's not about outsmarting the teacher; it's about being ready to deliver the intellectual goods.

This is especially true in the workplace. Anticipate what is needed; know more than what is expected. Pay attention over time to the kinds of questions being asked or the types of issues being discussed around the office. Be alert and aware so that you can pass those tests along the way, even the pop quizzes, one of which I failed one day.

Even for the Pentagon, the room was cavernous. It looked out onto the Tidal Basin and the Washington Monument. As the world's largest and longest office building—at that time with some 25,000 employees occupying offices along 17.5 miles of corridor—it had lots of important occupants.

I found myself on that fall afternoon sitting next to one of them, General John A. Wickham, Jr., the thirty-first U.S. Army chief of staff. The four-star general was being prepped for an upcoming press interview that in large part was my doing because I had recommended it, but the larger part of my responsibility was to help manage the outcome.

Sitting around the table were a half dozen general officers, another colonel, and myself. Subject-matter experts in everything from operational matters to logistical considerations, the two- and three-star generals were savvy in their respective fields and had come armed with data. They appeared confident and prepared for any question the chief might have.

Having advocated that the chief, as the senior uniformed officer in the army, be more aggressive in telling the army's story to stakeholders, I was pleased with the moment, for he was being prepped for a press interview the next day with a defense reporter from the *Washington Post.*

The staff members around the table were preparing him well. That was the case until the conversation shifted to whether one of General Wickham's initiatives might come up during the interview. He had recently decided that every soldier would identify with a unit in which he or she had served by wearing the crest of that unit on his or her uniform. The objective was to instill in the post-Vietnam generation a sense of purpose with a prideful allegiance to a unit of choice.

My battalion at Fort Carson, Colorado, in 1978–1979, the 1st Battalion, 12th Infantry, was my unit of choice. It had a rich history and tradition. I wore that unit's crest proudly on my uniform.

Midway through the discussion of the various issues that might be discussed in the interview, General Wickham turned to me and asked if his pet-rock unit designation scheme might come up. "Doubt it, sir," I said.

To optimize the mood of the moment, he asked me what my regimental designation was. After I told him, he asked the teachable moment question as he surveyed the crest I was wearing above my uniform pocket.

"What's the red, white, and blue on your crest stand for?" the general asked. An unforgettable memory as I stammered through my best guess, as opposed to what I should have known for certain.

"Actually," said the chief, "the white signifies purity, the red hardiness and valor, the blue vigilance, perseverance, and justice." Good deductive reasoning would have served me better than what

I had given him, but what I got in return was a "listen and learn" lesson.

Clearly I had been thinking more about the peaks than the valleys with respect to issues. It's the entire landscape that counts.

As I left this historic office that had been occupied by the likes of Generals John Pershing, George Marshall, Dwight Eisenhower, Omar Bradley, Matthew Ridgway, Maxwell Taylor, and William Westmoreland, I sensed that a takeaway lesson of life was to always think beyond the moment, that is, to consider what can or will happen next. We can or should plan for anything at any time, and that certainly includes satisfying the boss's questions or needs as they arise.

Back in my office I promised myself that from that point forward I'd prepare better both myself and my boss for the everything and anything in life. I would try always to know more than what was expected.

As the chief of media relations for the army at the time, I needed to know a lot about a lot of things. I began to construct my thoughts and actions in a way that allowed me, indeed forced me, to think beyond the horizon.

I vowed to anticipate the many things for me and my boss that could not only survive the moment but conquer the moment with my best advice and counsel. The boss may not ask for or expect it, I thought, but he surely needs and deserves it.

That doesn't happen by luck or by chance. It occurs because you acquire the knowledge. Become a consumer of information. Read for purpose and pleasure. Have an appetite for the news, both print and broadcast. Read at least two newspapers a day, local and national editions. Watch the local and national news on television. Listen to National Public Radio. Subscribe to industry publications. Attend conferences and workshops. Stay on top of things going on in the community, the business world, and the world at large. Simply know more than is expected. You'll be glad you did.

5

Anticipate What the Boss Wants or Needs

Most bosses set the organizational success bar to the desired height, and their expectation is that the rank and file will reach whatever that might be. That can lead to mission accomplishment, which is fine unless the boss is demanding and expects more than what has been asked for.

One way to achieve expectations or, better yet, to exceed them is to anticipate what the boss wants or needs. If your boss is not particularly demanding, he or she may ask for little or nothing. However, if expectations and demands are high, you need to be thinking ahead.

Having worked for many bosses with high standards, I became accustomed to anticipating what needed to be done. Not thinking ahead is what derails the train of progress.

Too often in our work life we suffer from a failure of imagination; in other words, we do not think the unthinkable. Let your imagination wander so that you think of all the things that could possibly go wrong on a project or with a plan. Map them, analyze them, and determine how to deal with them. Even if missteps never happen, you have anticipated the worst and probably can achieve the best.

Provide imaginative, creative thinking to the boss before decisions are made or actions are taken. This can elicit what the boss expects you or others to do to work through the issue. Always provide more detail or information than the boss may be expecting. Your thoughts cost nothing and may save money down the road.

You can also be an effective buffer or go-between for those things the boss either doesn't want to or doesn't have time to deal with. If the boss allows it, take charge of a project or a process that reflects favorably on the boss and at the same time is important for a successful outcome.

In the preparations for the first Gulf War, which began in January 1991, there were endless decisions that had to be made to get ready for the largest military operation since the Vietnam conflict. Generals Powell and Schwarzkopf had much to consider to get things right.

One consideration that gained their attention was the need to explain our military intentions and operational decisions to the various stakeholders involved. Both veterans of Vietnam, they understood well the critical importance of gaining and maintaining public approval for our actions, something we had failed to do in Vietnam. They chose not to repeat that calamitous error.

The late Arthur Page was the vice president of public relations for AT&T for 19 years in the 1930s and 1940s. Known today as the dean of the public relations profession, he earned that title for many principles that are hallmarks in the profession today. One thing Page said that fit the Gulf War requirements was, "All business in a democratic society begins with public approval." How true.

Public approval was what we sought. As chairman of the Joint Chiefs of Staff, General Powell had overall responsibility for the conduct of the war. As central command commander, General Schwarzkopf had operational responsibilities. Those responsibilities had to match.

After they had a powwow, General Powell summoned me to his office in December 1990. He told me that when the war commenced there would be a series of daily press conferences: one in the morning in Saudi Arabia and the other in the afternoon in Washington. He said, "Secretary Cheney and I will do some of the lifting, but I intend to ask Tom Kelly and Mike McConnell to do the bulk of it here in the Pentagon." Kelly was the three-star J3 operations officer for the Joint Staff; McConnell was the one-star J2 intelligence officer. Together they would know as much as if not more about friendly and enemy forces on the ground than anyone else.

By the time the war began on January 17, 1991, we had a plan in place. The next morning, Secretary of Defense Cheney and General Powell conducted the initial press conference in a Pentagon briefing room full of reporters. They did a masterful job. Our mission was under way to keep the many key stakeholders informed. They included the American people, Congress, the heads of state of international partners, the men and women in uniform, and, perhaps the most important of all, Saddam Hussein. A coalition of some 34 countries had been cobbled together to participate in the allied operation. It was crucial to keep them in the game with operational information.

Powell had directed me to work with Kelly and McConnell to develop both the style and the substance of the daily press conferences once the operation began. They were easy to support and eager to do what I recommended.

Since the daily press conference in Riyadh was going to be held at 10:00 a.m. EST, I recommended that ours be at 3:30 p.m. in the Pentagon. I told them I would prepare a list of anticipated questions each day by noon. We agreed to meet at 1:30 p.m. to wargame their answers.

Upon arrival at my Pentagon office each morning, I began to assemble likely questions. They were based on news reports over the last 24 hours, and I would add questions curious reporters would ask me in my office that day before noon. My crack staff helped me with that process. I would stop to watch the press conference from Riyadh, courtesy of CNN.

Typically, I'd have the 35 or more questions delivered to Kelly and McConnell by noon. They were educated guesses, but for the most part they resembled what was to come. At the appointed hour, I'd meet the general and the admiral in Kelly's office. They would assemble experts from their respective staffs to provide them with as much detail as necessary.

This process had been coordinated in advance with the assistant secretary of defense for public affairs for Secretary Cheney, Pete Williams. An exceptionally sharp professional, Pete would convene the press conference and provide details of his own to reporters after the two officers gave the briefing.

By day 3 of the war, a horde of reporters had assembled for the daily ritual. They grew in number to more than 200. Many were from international news organizations. Kiddingly, we used to describe many of them as the equivalent of food editors. Some knew little or nothing about national security. That made the challenge even greater for the briefers.

The war lasted 43 days. The air campaign accounted for the bulk of the operation; the ground phase lasted only 100 hours. Throughout the war, we held 38 press conferences in the Pentagon. We managed to gain and maintain public approval as Arthur Page had advocated. Only once, when I felt it start to falter, did I recommend that the chairman step in along with Mr. Cheney to get us back on track, and they did.

It was a memorable lesson of life: anticipate, assess, plan, and execute. Staying a step ahead of Colin Powell and others I worked with was indeed a challenge, but I vowed to never let them down. You won't get paid any more for anticipating what the boss may need, but you will be richer knowing that you did everything you could and should have to get the job done.

Anticipating for someone who already is your boss is hard enough. Anticipating for a new boss and someone you don't know yet is even more challenging. Rather than waiting until the new boss arrives to set that bar, reach out to the boss's current staff or colleagues. Ask the right questions of a chief of staff or a special assistant for the boss-to-be.

My new assistant-to-be as I transitioned from government to academia did her research well. She investigated everything down to the simple things such as my liking and using No. 2 pencils.

What is he like as a person? What are his management routines? What are his customs and habits? What can I anticipate him wanting or needing? Voilà! She had it down by the time I got there. It was seamless. It probably lowered her temperature to know in advance, and it certainly raised my spirits when I got there.

6

It's About the Boss;
It's Not About You

A good test of trust is whether one does what's right when the boss isn't there. Another good test is representing the boss in a way he or she would be proud of.

As someone who competes first and foremost against himself, I don't find these tough tests. Over the years, when the boss wasn't in the office because he was on business travel, I conducted myself as if he were watching my every move. Why? Because it was about the boss and what I knew were his standards and expectations. It was not about me, his assistant.

The boss is not the boss just because there was no other person to appoint to the position. In a perfect world, the boss occupies that chair because he or she has earned the right to lead others. If the boss does this well, he or she will command the respect and loyalty of subordinates.

As Jack Welch says in his bestselling leadership book *Winning*, success is achieved by leaders who are known for their knowledge, self-confidence, fairness, initiative, influence, self-control, decisiveness, dignity, courage, and integrity. The very best leaders have strategic vision, core values, and obtainable objectives. They know how to delegate responsibility but not ultimate responsibility.

Not all bosses meet such high standards. During my first tour in Vietnam as an infantry captain, I was assigned as a member of

23

an eight-man advisory team. We were stationed in a fairly remote area of what was known as II Corps. We lived, ate, and fought alongside our South Vietnamese counterparts. The senior advisor of the team was a major. I was his deputy. The others included a first lieutenant and five enlisted men ranging in rank from master sergeant to corporal.

About once a month our boss, the major, would assemble us for his version of admonishment. He would tell us we were not being active enough on combat operations. More patrols, more ambushes, more time in the field with our counterparts, he would demand. After each dressing-down, he would disappear to the room in which he lived in our quarters, which was a French-era house. Not bad digs except for the lack of running water.

In response to his orders, we would head to the field; he would not. Granted, he was getting pressure from the next higher head-quarters to do more, but he set a poor example with his stay-at-home actions.

Morale was bad; attitudes among members of the team toward him were not healthy. I found that part of my job as the number two was to keep heads held high, keep them actively engaged in operations, and remind them who the boss was.

Ironically, on a night when the major did go out on a combat patrol with two other members of the advisory team and a South Vietnamese unit, those of us who stayed back in our quarters came under attack by the Viet Cong. He missed all the action, and the laugh was on him.

I, for one, learned many lessons from this advisory team experience. Certainly we all learned how *not* to lead, how *not* to manage, how *not* to inspire others to follow. Through it all, I never forgot that the boss was the boss even if he wasn't the best of leaders. It wasn't about us as individual members of the team. It wasn't about me as a soldier. It was in this case that the major called the shots. Sometimes you can learn much from things that others do poorly so that you will not replicate their bad behavior.

There's an old expression that people only do things that the boss inspects or checks. Wouldn't life be better if we did more than what was expected? Even better, wouldn't it be nice to complete more tasks and go above and beyond when the boss is away?

Life in the workplace would be best if every boss were an authentic leader, one who not only inspired those around him or her to do their best but brought people together around a shared purpose. If all bosses had a set of strong and true values, they would motivate all the people around them to be the best they could be.

To achieve such success a boss must continually build and upgrade the team. He or she must set an example for others to follow.

7

Treat Every Day as Game Day

Unlike a conditioned athlete who warms up before an exercise or an athletic competition, most people rely on their energy level or metabolic rate to start and survive the day. That's all well and good, but it's not good enough.

The world in which we are living is moving at warp speed with more challenges and changes than ever before. To keep up with all that lies before us, we need conditioning and we need capacity.

Conditioning comes with maintaining a pace that allows us to accomplish the most, reprioritize the rest, and prepare for the unexpected. Capacity is the ability to reach back and down to draw on extra strength and resources to keep performing as long as it takes to get the job done.

Whenever I think of meeting that objective, I liken it to participating in some form of vigorous athletic competition in which strength and skill come into play. Preparation has been accomplished, a game plan is in place, and the adjustments to the plan are made on the run. As in battle, no plan survives first contact with the enemy; in the workplace, the same is true with the unexpected challenges and requirements that come along each day. Successful athletic teams rise to the occasion when the time clock starts and the score is kept. You need to do the same thing.

What's the value of being ready for prime time every day? The boss will love it. Bosses are always looking for the prime movers of their organization, the go-to men and women who get the job done first time, every time, and never miss a beat. That capacity to take on the known and the unknown is a priceless capability.

I had a full plate in the fall of 2010 both preparing for my next National Security Studies Program and teaching two public relations courses at Syracuse University, when my phone rang. It was Colonel Patrick Frank, commander of the Third Brigade Combat Team (3BCT) at Fort Drum, New York, an army installation an hour north of Syracuse. He said, "I'm taking my brigade to Afghanistan for a year's deployment next March, and I'm looking for a morale builder before we go, one that will work while we are in country." Pat told me that he was hoping to build a partnership with either the football or the basketball team at Syracuse University, an initiative that could boost and hold the spirit of his soldiers. Could I help? Caring a lot about soldiers and being a loyal follower of Orange athletic teams, I agreed to try. Why not both football and basketball? I asked. Pat enthusiastically agreed that two was better than one.

I called both football coach Doug Marrone and basketball coach Jim Boeheim. Without hesitating, they both said yes, they would be happy to partner with the brigade. It was easier to start with basketball, whose season had just begun. The football team was nearing the end of its season.

Colonel Frank and I met with coach Boeheim in December. Coach couldn't wait to get started. He offered to have 25 soldiers come for a basketball practice and dinner with the team on January 14, 2011. He also offered to provide 225 tickets to Fort Drum soldiers and families for a basketball game against Cincinnati in the Carrier Dome on January 15. A great start to the partnership.

By the time the 3,600 soldiers of the 3BTC deployed to Kandahar, Afghanistan, in March, a synergy had developed. During the tail end of the basketball season and into the next season for both football and basketball, soldiers in Afghanistan prepared "shout outs" for virtually every game. These "Go Orange" cheers were played on the big screens in the Carrier Dome and evoked standing ovations for our soldiers.

In March 2011 the partnership with the football team took shape. Members of the brigade's rear detachment came to campus to observe a practice in April, and in June a group of SU football players visited Fort Drum for "a day in a life of a soldier," which amounted to vigorous military-oriented training. The following October, 20 SU basketball players and six coaches visited Fort Drum for a similar day of training. In both cases, they experienced a teleconference with Colonel Frank in Afghanistan. Pat told the athletes what life was like in a combat zone and urged them on to successful seasons. Cool stuff for the kids.

The two relationships have matured and will continue into the future. The commonalities between soldiers and athletes are striking. In both cases, they thrive on competition, they practice leadership, they require teamwork, and they prepare for offense and defense.

Additionally, I arranged for a day of "Governance Training" at the Maxwell School at SU for senior leaders of the brigade before their deployment. They used best practices in dealing with Afghan government representatives. That training went so well that Colonel Frank asked for a tutorial for his staff in dealing with the media, and so I arranged for a day of "Media Training" at the Newhouse School at SU. They used that as well to tell their unit's story while in Afghanistan.

I took great pride in the fact that Syracuse University was the only school in the country that had built partnerships between both their football and their basketball teams and the same military unit. These collaborations were so newsworthy that John King of CNN aired a piece on Veterans Day 2011 featuring the Army-Syracuse connection.

Just when you think you have a full plate, you find that you have to add to it. When it's for a good cause like this one, you don't blink. But even when the causes and requirements aren't as scintillating, if it's important, it is a necessary thing to do.

In this case, the battlefield and the ball field came together, as did the soldiers and the athletes. In the everyday workplace often it's the busiest person who is asked to do the additional and toughest jobs. Those who do are burdened by it but can be blessed by it too, for they learn and grow faster than their peers.

Does the boss even see or notice these things? Absolutely! This is when your capacity and conditioning and ability to treat every day as a game day are valued and admired by the person who has put you in the game. Success will be your reward.

8

Manage the Calendar and the Clock

Two lines from the rock band Chicago's 1970 hit song of the same name say it all. "Does anybody really know what time it is? Does anybody really care?" The answer to both questions too often is no, they don't.

I found I had to. Being a 23-year-old first lieutenant company commander at Fort Benning, the sprawling home of the U.S. Army Infantry School in Columbus, Georgia, was fairly overwhelming. The responsibility for over 450 men was more than I had bargained for. Full days, some nights managing my unit. There was hardly enough time in a day to do it all.

Thinking I'd be clever and find ways to save time reading all that was put before me in the office in-box, I enrolled in a speed-reading class conducted by a Columbus College professor. It was conveniently held on post at Fort Benning. The first night of the course the professor asked some 30 of us gathered in a classroom, "What's your most important resource in life?" In line with the type of course and trying to sound smart, I guessed my eyes and the vision they provided. Each of us got to answer; each of us was wrong. "Time is your most important resource," announced the professor. His tutorial on the importance of time and how to save it has always remained with me.

Time management has become almost an obsession for me: determining how to manage time, assessing how to spend it, having a plan to do what needs to get done, doing it wisely, and evaluating how it's been done.

The more time you have in which to serve your boss, to do your job, to manage the missions that come your way, the better off you will be. If you fail to do it well, you will not fulfill the expectations the boss has of you. Keep time on your side and find ways to maximize it.

For example, how do you spend the first 15 minutes of the day? Heading to the watercooler or coffeepot? Shooting the breeze about sports or shopping or what you're going to do this weekend? Nice to do socially but not very effective professionally. You're better off firing up your computer and getting down to business when you first get to your desk in the morning. Have that last cup of coffee while at home or in the car.

Statistically, we tend to work in increments of time. Scheduling tasks that take more than 30 minutes of your time may defy what experts believe. Break up your day into segments.

You need to prioritize because it is unlikely you will finish what you set out to do. Generally, you will accomplish about 65 percent of what's on your to-do list each day. You will need to reprioritize for tomorrow the tasks not done today and those yet to do tomorrow.

How do you spend the most productive two hours of the day, the second and third? If you're busy talking unnecessarily or meeting aimlessly, you aren't spending it wisely.

When it comes to those meetings, you need to set the clock. Unless it's handling a crisis, any meeting that lasts more than 30 minutes is too long. If you have some control over a meeting, there are ways to keep it in check. Establish an agenda, circulate it in advance, keep attendees to a minimum, and ask that everyone come prepared. Another rule that works is to shut the door and lock it for those who don't make it on time. Amazingly, that breeds punctuality.

As difficult as it may be for Type A personalities, it pays to delegate. It saves time, it spreads the workload, and it even builds teamwork. Don't feel you can or have to do it all.

Having a plan is a useful approach to the management of your day. Making a morning appointment with yourself whether in the shower or in the car or when you first arrive at the office is a useful beginning.

Have a five-minute meeting at the top of the day with your assistant if you have one. You may have added chores for the day to your list. Keep in balance scheduled versus unscheduled activities. Do not try to accomplish more than is possible. Reorder your priorities as need be.

The implementation part of your day is perhaps the most difficult. Start and end things on time. Block those productive second and third hours against invasion. Be gracious but ruthless with those who try to invade your time and space. Keep a drop-in standing rather than offering them a seat. Always set the outer limits of appointments and meetings. No appointment should last more than 30 minutes; 15 is better yet.

Deadlines are critical to all this. You need to meet them, and in order to do so, you need to have a low procrastination quotient. Work on eliminating one if you have it.

Evaluating each day in terms of the degree of progress you are making is a useful monitoring device. As part of this evaluation process, elicit feedback from your team. Discuss successes and failures with yourself and your staff. In doing this, ask open-ended questions. When you ask a question that begs an answer, let someone else do the talking.

If you have done all these things as well as you can, you're bound to be productive. Think of all the beneficiaries: certainly yourself but the boss, too, and don't forget the folks who work for you. Having time for your most important stakeholder group, your employees, is a gift they will treasure. The boss will value it too.

9

Never Wear Your Boss's Rank or Position

"Oh, Lord, it's hard to be humble." So goes the song. Too often people of high importance don't show humility. They brag, they name-drop, they exaggerate far beyond their position in life. To use an old expression, we all put our pants on the same way. I wish we all could act that way.

This attitude of deserving special treatment can extend to people who work for people of high importance. Yes, there are people who think their boss is so important, so special, so incredible that they deserve special attention by virtue of association. When that attention reverts to misrepresentation, especially when the boss doesn't know it's happening, it becomes a problem.

Aides, executive assistants, secretaries—the title doesn't matter—can exceed the authority and the responsibilities vested in them by speaking for the boss without his or her permission. Power is corrupting; ultimate power is ultimately corrupting. It is corrupting in the sense that you exceed your rights and responsibilities by misrepresenting the facts or the truth.

When three officials of a foreign country registered for my National Security Studies Program, I was excited—that is, until the assistant at the particular country's embassy in Washington, D.C., jumped in and asked for special treatment for her three VVIPs, as she called them. They needed billeting at the Ritz-Carlton in Syracuse. We don't have one, we replied. They needed to be picked up and transported to class each morning in a Mercedes, she said. They didn't need one; they could walk to campus with other participants, was our response.

Our policy is to leave rank at the door; everyone is a VVIP to us. When the three participants arrived weeks later, they had no knowledge of all the special requests. They were more than happy with their accommodations at the Sheraton University Hotel & Conference Center right on campus, and they happily walked to class with the other participants.

When I booked a senior government official to speak to one of the classes, I never anticipated how hard it would be to get her to her destination. Direct flights from Washington, D.C., to Syracuse are many, quick, and convenient. That didn't work for this particular person's secretary, who booked her, at our expense, from Washington to Detroit to Syracuse because she thought it was a better choice. Counterarguments did not prevail. When the official finally arrived weeks later, she could not understand how hard it had been for her to get to Syracuse. When we explained the circumstances to her, she was shocked. She had never been provided the options by her secretary.

After a brigadier general registered for one of my courses, my assistant began dealing with her assistant, who demanded special arrangements the general needed and required. They included special accommodations, special meals, a special bed, and the list went on. We thought we had a prima donna on our hands. When the brigadier arrived, we braced ourselves for the worst. It was not the case. Upon being asked if all the special accommodations were in order, she said, "There goes my secretary again. She does this all the time, and I never request or need any special treatment."

I'm all for special strokes for special folks because they deserve them, not because they demand them. It's extremely devious for an assistant to wear the boss's rank or position when it is not required.

First off, it makes the principal seem like a demon before you meet him or her, when in fact he or she has been misrepresented.

When General Powell asked me to retire with him, I arranged for a suite of offices for us. We retired on a Thursday, the last day in September. The next day I set up shop. I filled the three rooms with furniture, phones, and office equipment. When I shut the door that Friday afternoon, I was feeling pretty smug.

The following Monday I opened that same door to an eerie sound: the sound of silence. No staff, no support structure, no one but myself to talk and give orders to.

It may sound flattering to be the only employee for one of the most respected men in the nation, but it actually seemed more scary than special. Why? Because every phone call answered, every letter written, every request received had to be handled with dignity and class. He expected it, and I felt a responsibility to provide it.

There were dozens of opportunities a day to speak for him and represent him in the most responsible, authentic way. It would have been easy to exceed that authority. It would have been tempting to misrepresent that responsibility. He still had rank even though he was retired, and he still had position by virtue of his respectability and popularity. I vowed to myself never to wear that rank or position in his stead.

Popularized by Mario Puzo's 1969 novel *The Godfather*, the term *consigliere* became a vogue word. It stood for an advisor or counselor to the boss in Mafia crime families. That person had the additional responsibility of representing the boss in important meetings or conversations within the boss's crime family or with another crime family. A close, trusted confidant, that person had voice and power. That power can be exercised in a book, in a movie adaptation, or in real life. How it is used or misused is the issue.

You too may be a consigliere or counselor to the boss. And with that comes the power that reflects that person's rank or position. You can do that best by knowing what the boss *really* needs, wants, or expects. You should communicate those things in the most honest, accurate way, never embellished but always within reason. Not too hard, not too soft, just right.

Every interaction you have with others on behalf of your boss leaves an impression, good or bad, right or wrong. It's also an impression of you as someone dedicated to the boss's needs but one who wants both the boss and the other party to look good. If you do it the proper way, it will turn out to be the right way.

10

Never Allow Your Boss
to Be Surprised

In your professional life as in your private life, things don't always go right. In fact, things can go very wrong, and when they do, obviously something needs to be done about it.

In the business world, responsibilities and resources include people, money, equipment, infrastructure, and technology. Breakdown can occur in any of these areas. People make mistakes, profits are down, equipment gets broken, infrastructure needs repair, and technology goes haywire.

This may be particularly problematic when a crisis occurs, and rest assured it will. A lot of bosses operate from a position of denial: "Can't happen here." "We're too good." "Not on my watch." Actually, it's not a matter of if but when a crisis will occur.

If you find or see a problem, you have some choices: run the other way, keep quiet about it, hope it goes away, or do what's best and report it. To whom? To the next in charge so that that person and subsequent individuals of responsibility can take it up the chain of command.

Unfortunately, when it comes to telling the big boss, that process is often interrupted. Some attempt to solve the problem before the boss finds out. Others are simply afraid to let the boss know there's a problem to begin with.

Smart bosses want to know when something is wrong. Only then can they do something about it.

Some organizations are fortunate enough to have risk or quality control officers, people who can serve as a conscience for an organization. Actually, people up and down the line should be looking for things that aren't right, and when they find something wrong, there ought to be a willingness to take the problem to the top.

Not long after Colin Powell became chairman of the Joint Chiefs of Staff, I recognized that there was a growing problem that was about to erupt. It was a national security matter I felt he should know more about in terms of information, quite frankly, that reporters had shared with me. I drafted a memorandum that I sent down to the front office for his review and consideration.

The next day I got a call from his personal secretary to say that the chairman wanted to see me. I hastened down to the front office, only to be met by several staff members who had gathered in anticipation. One of them said, "I think you're in trouble." "Why so?" I asked. The answer was "I don't think he liked what you had to say." When I asked what he meant by that, he pointed to the upper right corner of the memo and said, "See the BS which the chairman has written here? He thinks it's bullshit!"

I came to find out that that was the way the general indicated the disposition of correspondence. He would put the initials of the intended recipient where they could be plainly seen. Not knowing that at the moment, I entered the chairman's office uncertain about my fate.

I said, "Sir, you wanted to see me about this?" I handed him the memo. He asked several questions beyond what I had put on paper. He thanked me for alerting him to the situation. He then said, "Keep an eye on this and keep me informed." I was relieved to know that the initials stood for my name, not the boss's wrath.

I didn't take advantage of the outcome by becoming the town crier, but I was never afraid to let the boss know when something wrong was brewing. That way I was assured he would never be surprised.

Even if you can fix the problem, it's still a problem, and most likely the boss deserves to know. A likely benefit that can occur from not allowing the boss to be surprised is that confidence in you is bound to grow. The relationship is destined to grow stronger. You might even become a confidant.

It's not that you have to become a spy for the boss, but you could find that the boss will come to depend on you more and more. Actually, the true beneficiary is the organization at large.

In the old days a frequently heard saying was "He's a company man." It meant someone who was reliable, someone who was trustworthy, someone who always did the right thing. It was a term of endearment. Being a company man or a company woman in today's world means the same thing. Part of that attribute is taking care of business, and part of taking care of business is never letting the boss be surprised.

11

Never Sign the Boss's Signature

Theft is an unfortunate and unpleasant occurrence. Whether you're the villain or the victim, you are on the wrong side of a bad habit. If you have been the perpetrator of the theft, you have committed a wrong; if you are the victim, you have been wronged. When personal property is stolen, that is a painful experience; when personal identity is stolen, that is an improper misuse of one's property.

When I was younger, the only thing I had responsibility for with regard to providing my signature were things such as term papers and automobile registrations. Nothing terribly dramatic.

My first assignment in the army was as a second lieutenant of infantry in the Republic of Korea. Suddenly the magnitude of putting my signature to documents increased dramatically. As a platoon leader, I had responsibility for the 44 men who were assigned to me. The equipment the platoon needed to operate—things such as armored personnel carriers, trucks, and jeeps—was a different matter. I had to sign for all of that as the senior member of the platoon. Millions of dollars' worth of equipment.

I recall the supply sergeant warning me, "Lieutenant, you lose it, you buy it." The stakes had suddenly gone up. I recognized that I needed to take this act of using my signature more seriously than ever before.

I will never forget a fellow lieutenant who had similarly signed for his platoon property. When it came time to turn things back in to the supply system when he was scheduled to rotate home, he found that he was missing a building he had signed for a year earlier. "How could that happen?" he asked. "How could I lose a building?" The answer was simple: he hadn't counted what he was signing for, and he signed for it without thinking much about it. He bought the building. That was a tough lesson in life for him. For me it was an unforgettable lesson to always bear in mind.

Signing for things happened routinely throughout my professional career. It became a more important act with time. I had to assume responsibility for lots of things. Over time, the relevance of my signature became more significant. I took it more seriously and never allowed anyone to sign my name to something for which I had responsibility.

But as I went from place to place throughout my career, I saw many people sign everything from letters of recommendation, to memos, to equipment vouchers for others, mostly superiors, without their permission. As I saw it, this was like borrowing or stealing someone's property.

The consequences of such an act hit home when a boss for whom I worked in more senior days found that an assistant had signed his name to a document without asking his permission. He went ballistic. If you think about it, he had every right to react that way. He made it patently clear to members of the staff that not only was it an improper act, it should never happen again. As I moved along in my assignments, I saw it happen more often than it should have.

Fortunately, I have a signature that is fairly distinctive and would be difficult to replicate. Interestingly, several assistants admitted they had tried to forge my signature but couldn't come close to matching it. In each case, I told them they were lucky to have failed and to never try again. Being overly conscious of the ramifications of someone signing a document for me caused me to be diligent about it not happening.

In an age in which it is possible to scan one's signature and send things electronically, it's even easier to misappropriate the use of one's name. Only with permission have I ever allowed that to happen. I have made it very clear to my assistants that before they use my scanned signature, they need to verbally ask me for permission. Each and every time. No exceptions!

Even if the boss gave me permission to have his signature applied in his absence, I'd find another way. It's not right, and it's a misuse of one's personal and intellectual property that simply should not happen.

Over the course of time, I have routinely signed my name several thousand times each year. Sure, it took time. Sure, it was an extra step. But it represented something very important to me. It should also be important to you and to your boss to do things the right way.

12

Get a Seat at the Table

As a child, did you ever get invited to a holiday dinner at Grandma's and hope to get seated at the table with the grownups but instead were banished to another room with the rest of the kids? It's an especially disappointing and even lonely feeling when you're left out of the adults' talk, especially when you think you can contribute to the conversation.

It's not too different, if you think about it, to be excluded from the executive table at work when you just might benefit from hearing what your managers and even your peers who did get invited have to say. The question is, How do you gain and, more important, maintain a proverbial seat at the table?

A starting point is to know as much about your organization or subject matter as there is to know. What are its core competencies? What does its strategic plan include? Who are the stakeholders? What business relationship is in play with each stakeholder group? What contracts exist, and which ones are being pursued? What products are on-line or in production? What is the revenue picture, and what needs to happen for the outlook to improve? What are the future ventures that require attention?

Once you have assembled that information in your data bank, there are questions you need to ask yourself: What can I do to prove I can make a contribution to the discussions being conducted regarding these issues or causes? How might that lend itself to business results?

That doesn't mean an offer will be extended to you overnight. It may take time to build your reputation. There are ways to do that. If you have a report to write, is it well thought out and written? If you are developing a strategy, does it have substance and worth? If you're asked a question by a middle manager in the hallway, do you have a ready answer that makes sense? Opportunities to demonstrate your value to the organization can happen at any time. Be ready to make an impact.

Yes, it starts with educating yourself so that you have a true understanding of the challenges, the initiatives, and the successes of the company. Be so familiar with the strategy of the organization that your actions complement whatever the goals are. Speak the language that echoes that strategy. In everything you do strive to be a true professional.

Gaining that seat at the table is not a gift. It is earned. You're not invited just to warm a chair. You're there to show you have the right stuff.

It helps to look the part in the way you dress. My philosophy is to always dress up. That entails being the best-dressed person in the room: a well-tailored suit or dress, a starched shirt or blouse, a sharp tie or an elegant scarf. Not too many bangles and beads but enough to set your attire off. Take pride in the way you look. If you find others looking at you, there is probably a reason. It may be how well you are dressed.

It may also be because you're prepared for the meeting. If an agenda has been published, research each and every item. Come prepared with relevant knowledge and expertise. That's important if the boss turns to you and you're able to provide thoughtful, well-reasoned views or advice.

For me, getting a seat at the table came in my first assignment as a second lieutenant in the Republic of Korea. My captain company commander called me in after he had been there only two months. He said, "Lieutenant, I intend to put higher emphasis on training and how it's conducted. I am assigning you the additional duty of training officer for the company." I was one of a handful of lieutenants in the company of 250 soldiers, and he could have chosen any one of us for this duty, but he picked me. It was a lot of extra work, but I learned so much from having to develop a weekly training schedule, select the subjects, and assign the instructors. Dialogue with the captain over what to do and how to do it was constant.

It went well enough that after two months had passed he called me in to say, "You're doing a good enough job as training officer that I'm going to let you deploy the company to the field and conduct the training there." That was a huge deal. Moving men and machines long distances, creating realistic training scenarios, supervising the details of the exercise, and evaluating the training results were significant undertakings. I must have done it well enough because at the 7-month mark of my 13-month tour I was elevated to battalion headquarters as the only lieutenant chosen to be the assistant operations officer.

Later in my army career, as a special assistant to two chairmen of the Joint Chiefs of Staff, I was invited to attend the morning staff meetings in the National Military Command Center. The room was filled with enough stars to light up a galaxy. The generals and admirals sat around the highly polished conference table. Yes, I was a backbencher, one of four without stars but with special status. It was a unique privilege that allowed me to hear discussions on issues of high importance to the nation. It was not uncommon for Admiral Crowe or General Powell to turn to me and ask for my opinion on something being discussed.

This went a long way toward building my credibility as a source the chairman valued. It also went a long way toward building relationships with all the directors who were responsible for running the Joint Staff. They too would come to me for advice, and I in turn was able to count on them, with the permission of the chairman, to give speeches and interviews on his behalf. This carte blanche privilege accomplished many things that otherwise would not have happened. Credibility is a powerful tool.

Your skill and competence are your tools for gaining that recognition as a resource that is highly valued. Once you gain a seat at that all-important table, you are a full-fledged member of the team. You'll know that you've made it when the boss seeks your advice and wisdom and other people at the table turn to listen to what you have to say.

Having a seat at the table can extend beyond the boardroom. When a senior manager calls you or comes to visit to get your advice on something, that's an extension of the seat you've earned. On a spur of the moment or routine basis, you need to be prepared to be that go-to person whom people rely on for your judgment and opinions. Once you do this, you will find that it's a great place to be.

13

Pace Yourself and Your Boss

There are going to be dark days. There are going to be dog days. There are going to be days when you are not sure you will make it through the day or night.

Just when you think you are at the breaking point, look around. How are your teammates doing? Most important, how's your boss doing? If the answer to those questions is "not well," it's time to reach down and pull yourself up by your bootstraps, and them as well.

I'm not sure who told me or taught me. Maybe I figured it out for myself. No matter what the source, the ritual I have grown to believe in and have been able to rely on whenever the going gets tough is to find capacity. The capacity to do what? To push back the fatigue, to wipe away tired eyes, and to find the means to let the adrenaline kick in so that I can do the job no matter how long it takes or how tough it is.

There are going to be times of crisis when that extra dose of energy is essential. When the clock strikes one and you are only halfway there, you need to find that lift. There are energy bars and energy drinks that may help. Better yet, the inner strength that each of us has needs to be developed and tried.

At the center of such times in your professional life is someone who needs you more than you know: your boss. Some bosses cry out for help; others let out not a whimper. Does that mean, in the

51

first case, that they definitely need a boost from you? Most likely. In the second instance, does it mean that there are telltale signs you should be looking for? Always.

Pacing yourself is one way to eliminate or alleviate a situation in which you feel you've lost control. The best way to do that is to start and stop things on time. If you let the events of the day pile up or run into one another, you're bound to have a problem. It may be that either you or your boss needs prodding. Get over it; get on with it. But stay on schedule and maintain a pace that is prescribed and programmed. There needs to be someone to keep the clock and keep things moving on time.

I once knew a senior defense official who was a workaholic. Actually, there are many of them wearing the uniform of our nation. This one, however, was a fanatic. He insisted that the first briefing of the day be given to him at 5:30 a.m., or 0-dark-30, which in Pentagonese means "very darn early!" Nothing ever ended on time. Briefers were stacked up in the outer office and eventually in the hallway. Those who had to brief this admiral went to bed in fear, woke up in fear, and walked the briefing plank in fear. This had no semblance of order or discipline. And shame on any assistant who tried to restore normality.

I was fortunate never to have worked for such a demanding and undisciplined sort. However, I've had ample opportunity to work for people who could cram more into a day than the next three people.

While on the chairman's staff, I could count on being part of a delegation that would attend a quarterly NATO meeting in Brussels, Belgium. The good news was that there were mussels to be had at the end of the workday. The bad news was the travel aspect of the trip. Often, we would leave on a Sunday afternoon just in time to miss a good ball game so that we would arrive at NATO headquarters the next morning just in time to go to the first meeting. On the return leg that Thursday, we would land at Andrews Air Force Base in Maryland around 7 a.m., just in time to be taken by helicopter to the Pentagon to start the workday.

Eventually, we persuaded the chairman to arrive in Brussels early enough Monday morning to take a two- to three-hour nap. He agreed to the new pace. It worked well for him, and the staff was delighted with the new sequence, which kept us fresh throughout the day.

In the next stage of life with General Powell—private life—the pace did not lessen. In fact, we retired on a Thursday, and on Friday I found myself setting up our private offices with furniture, fax, phone, and computer. I did take the weekend off, but we started our new life early Monday morning with the beginning stages of writing his book.

We set a pace that was reasonable and achievable. From October 1993 until Fourth of July weekend 1995, we picked away at assembling the words and the wisdom encompassed in what would become his bestselling autobiography.

Then came the editing of the book by a talented writer and editor who scoured the manuscript for detail and comprehension. This was followed by the publishing of the book by Random House.

Come that September, the pace changed. We embarked on what I affectionately called the mother of all book tours. He and I were off and running on a five-week marathon doing book signings and press interviews. We knew that the road ahead would be trying, so we developed a plan. Part of that plan was taking advantage of the offer by the chairman of the banking company MBNA to lend us a corporate jet. It sure beat commercial air travel and probably saved our hides.

We also agreed that between the departure each Monday morning and the return each Friday evening we needed a healthy routine, a nutritional diet, no alcohol, and lots of sleep. It worked. The only things worn out at the end of each week were the suits we took with us.

Not everyone has such control over his or her destiny. Those who do need to maintain a disciplined schedule and pace for themselves and the boss. Those who don't need to get a grip.

If you are in that category, this may start with a conversation you may want to have with the boss. Ask the question out loud: How can we do a better job of being in control of where we are going and how we are going to get there? The right answer can benefit you both.

14

Provide the Boss Some Quiet Time Each Workday

Most people feel fortunate if they survive the day and accomplish all the things that are required of them. That's fine, but it's not sufficient if it appears to be difficult for you to take on anything extra. Think about how it might be for your boss, who has tons more to do over the course of the workday than most in his or her employ.

What's the solution for you and your boss if that is the case? It's to carve out time whether you have it or not. To do what? To think. To plan. To strategize. If you think about it, your boss needs to do that too. For that to happen the staff needs to carve out some kind of zone of privacy for the boss.

Strategic thinking is essential in this day and age. Six months out, two years out, a decade from now. What should you and the boss be thinking about with respect to your organizational future and what it holds?

Quiet time is important time, and if you don't take it, you lose it to something else.

When could that be during a busy day? Not in the morning. That's the busiest time for most people. It could be at noon in line or connection with lunch in the privacy of an office or in a quiet corner. Or it could be in some part of the afternoon when things slow down.

The challenge is that chief executives aren't in control of their day and how they spend it. The London Business School of Economics and the Harvard Business School surveyed 500 chief executive officers and found that, in a 55-hour workweek, they were trapped doing things that were far from fun.

In an average workweek for those executives, 18 hours were spent in meetings, 2 making phone calls, 2 on conference calls, 2 in public events, 5 having business meals, and 20 participating in miscellaneous activities. Only 6 hours were spent working alone.

When Colin Powell became secretary of state in January 2001, he became one of the busiest people in the country. He had bilateral meetings, countless visitors, and myriad phone calls. Never a dull moment, never a spare moment, so it seemed.

As his chief of staff and someone who took responsibility for his workday, I issued an ultimatum to the staff: the secretary gets quiet time in the amount of an hour a day unless he's on travel or there is a crisis at hand.

It made no difference what time of day; however, it made a difference that he had the time. To do what? To go on his computer and get information, to pick up a phone and gather information or give direction to others, or simply to stare out the window and think.

He not only came to value that quiet time, he came to expect it. It was something we put on his calendar of the day's activities, and people protected it. They even enjoyed it, and the smart ones took time for themselves during the time we fenced for him.

How to make this routine? Declare it and do it. What's the value of all this? For one thing, it is bound to reenergize you mentally and physically. At the end of the day it makes you feel more confident that you have planned or assessed something that otherwise might not have happened.

It can be a hands-behind-the-head moment. It could be scribbling notes to yourself, it could even be doodling or googling something you were looking for. But whatever it is or whatever you make it, it's apt to make you better at what you do.

There's a lot of sense to that. If it's good for you, think of what you are doing for the boss. That person of importance in your professional life needs and deserves this quiet time too.

If the boss rejects the notion to formalize this habit, find a way to sell it. If nothing else, ask for a trial run. If you are successful, you may be on the road to a precious destination.

When I told the secretary's secretary to provide him with private time, I got a "Yahoo!" I thought she was going to dance around the office. She was more excited about this quiet time for the secretary of state than I had expected. She had never had this luxury for her previous bosses. If she had, I suspect she'd have been taking better care of them.

15

Send the Boss
on That Needed Vacation

When it comes to hard work, Americans tend to overindulge. They work too many hours, they work too many days, and they work too many weeks a year compared with their counterparts in other parts of the world.

That certainly helps when you are measuring gross domestic product or company profits. It's not so helpful when you are measuring fatigue or burnout.

It's particularly bad if the boss sets the standard extremely high when it comes to a work schedule. It can be especially bad when the term *vacation* is not part of the boss's vocabulary. I've worked for bosses who seemingly couldn't or wouldn't take the time to enjoy family or friends by slipping out of town occasionally to play.

The unfortunate part of a case in which the boss doesn't take the allotted vacation time is that the people who surround that boss keep the same nonstop schedule. They become self-imposed victims to workaholic tendencies.

If you find that you have two or three weeks of vacation each year but aren't able to take it, it may be a use-it-or-lose-it situation. You shouldn't let that kind of loss happen. You deserve whatever time you are given for vacation whether it's all at once or spread out over time. You deserve to take each day you are given.

If you find that the boss is the problem because you are expected to be there when the boss is there, it is probably time to have a conversation with the person for whom you work. If you have created the same expectation, you may want to have a conversation with yourself.

If this conversation yields no relief, you may want to find an ally or advocate for the vacation cause. What better person to have agree with you that a vacation is essential than the spouse, be it the boss's or your own?

I had many a boss who worked long, hard days. Those days seemed endlessly strung together so that time off was rare. In the military it is part of the culture. When I retired from the army and neither my boss nor I was tied to operational or crisis situations, we could think differently about how we spent our time.

I even found that my boss's wife had expectations of him that were different from the way he spent his time during his military days. I suggested to her that they needed time to enjoy family and friends in other parts of the country. She agreed. We began plotting. Before I knew it, they were enjoying the ability to get away. I found pleasure in that too. It was good for them; it was good for me.

What's the value of taking a deserved or a much-needed vacation? To begin with, you're apt to return to the workplace refreshed, even reenergized. You might have a whole new attitude toward what you do, how you do it, and why. The same thing applies to the boss.

Who are the beneficiaries? The staff, your colleagues, and the organization can all be rewarded. Most of all, your family may benefit.

Unfortunately, a lot of bosses are simply workaholics. They somehow believe the office can't manage without them when in fact it might actually be of benefit for the staff to have a break from the boss.

If you are of the mind that the boss can't survive without you, get over it. Life does not stop because you're not there. In fact, a simple thing such as a break from each other could actually act as therapy or be medicinal.

16

Keep the Boss's Better Half Informed and Involved

It had never really occurred to me that I had responsibilities beyond the needs of the boss at any particular moment, whatever that moment might be.

What a surprise at a particular teachable moment it was for me to realize that the boss's spouse counted too! And why not? Most of our spouses hold a fairly important and prominent place in our lives. Thus, when I failed to pay attention to that most important person in my boss's life, his wife, I learned the hard way that it's not wise to leave the spouse out—with information, with involvement, or even with deserved attention.

It was not long after General Powell became chairman of the Joint Chiefs of Staff that he was invited to a dinner event in downtown Washington at the Marriott Hotel. I had asked him to attend the event, which included Mrs. Powell as a guest as well. Members of his security detail met us at the front door of the hotel and swept us past the people gathered in the lobby. They took us straight to a reception area for cocktails and conversation. The Powells walked to the room together as I tagged behind, as it should be. When we reached the door of the reception room, the dynamics changed. He moved straight in with me at his side. It didn't take long for the two of us to be surrounded by dozens of invited guests who wanted to share in the moment.

It wasn't that he didn't have a sizable reputation that would naturally attract people to him. He had been the national security advisor to President Ronald Reagan, so he wasn't exactly an unknown figure in government. As we stood there surrounded by attendees, it seemed all was going well until I looked behind me and discovered that Alma Powell had been left out of the circle and the moment. If looks could kill, I knew I was in trouble, and in all likelihood my boss was as well.

I reached back, grabbed her hand, and pulled her forward into the circle. I apologized and whispered, "This will never happen again." And it didn't. Quite frankly, it strengthened our relationships: mine with her and mine with him.

She knew I respected her position, her prominence, and her participation. I promised myself never to repeat that omission. In fact, I thought long and hard about how to prevent it in the future.

Every time I sent a memo to him, I sent one to her. Every time I briefed him on what to expect, I briefed her. It was a family affair. Even if she didn't accompany him, she knew where he was, what he was doing, and when he would be home.

The boss might not think his or her spouse needs to know what's going on or whether he or she should be included. Your job is to think for your boss. Your job is to figure it out. Your job is to connect the dots.

Quite likely your boss will be grateful that you did it. And if that is the case, you have performed another good deed on behalf of the boss. If there is such a thing as pillow talk and if one-half of the relationship expresses appreciation that he or she was included, it just might make for a better day for your boss tomorrow.

17

Accompany the Boss on Business Travel

As I was standing on a pier on a Friday night at around 10:30 p.m. in Philadelphia, the view was breathtaking. The stars were out and seemed to dangle over the beautiful downtown skyline. I turned to the boss, Army Secretary John O. Marsh, Jr., and remarked, "Sir, we've got to stop meeting like this."

There had been many late workday nights on which I accompanied him as he did the business of the institution and the people. A former congressman, Jack Marsh was accustomed to working long days and nights. He had a penchant for doing the "extra" duties of his office at night and on weekends, never wanting to be far from the Pentagon during normal duty hours.

On this particular night, we had just come from a speech he had given at the historic Union Club in the City of Brotherly Love. At the moment, we were waiting for a helicopter to take us to the Philadelphia International Airport for a flight home.

There were so many other after-hours times with him, such as a scorching Saturday afternoon watching soldiers train at Fort Benning, Georgia. A Tuesday night in western Pennsylvania at a schoolhouse for a talk he was asked to give by Congressman Tom Ridge, a Vietnam veteran. A Wednesday afternoon and evening at Redstone Arsenal in Alabama when he was asked to speak to military and civilian representatives of the Huntsville area. A Friday evening in Charleston, West Virginia, at the invitation of Senator Jay Rockefeller to speak to citizens there about the state of the army. And countless more.

Taking care of the boss during times like these was a natural thing to do. The unnatural thing happened on the return trip from Charleston, West Virginia, to Fort Belvoir, Virginia, onboard an Army C-12 commuter plane. We were making our final descent to the military airport at Fort Belvoir when wind shear caught the plane and veered it hard right on a nearly 45-degree angle. Secretary Marsh was sitting one row forward to my left. I glanced over at him and sensed his concern. It mirrored mine. The two warrant officer pilots remained actively seized of the matter. They fought the controls and conditions and miraculously righted the aircraft just before touching down. I will never forget the secretary turning to me, relief in his eyes, and saying, "How about that!" The "that" was a Kodak moment, and it came with the territory of accompanying the boss on travel.

Beyond taking the responsibility for supporting the secretary or any of my bosses over the years for things I had asked them to do, they valued and expected someone to be by their side. To do what? To ensure that the details I had outlined in a pre-trip memo played out as expected.

Logistics are at the heart of any trip. This goes beyond just getting there and home. For me they included getting the boss comfortably settled in the commonly held reception scheduled beforehand while I went down the checklist of things I had requested in advance to confirm they were in order for the main event. That included everything: the room setting, the head table layout, who was seated at the right and left of the boss, whether the podium was lighted and had a slant with a lip, and whether the microphone was working properly. In a world in which PowerPoint presentations are common, the technology needs to be perfect. These things sound routine, but one should never leave anything to chance.

Most of my bosses had a protective habit when it came to their speeches. They resisted letting their speech box be out of their sight. Secretary Marsh was the most protective of all. He told me once that during his time as a congressman, he had put his speech on the podium in advance of being introduced. When he went to the podium to deliver his remarks, he found that the person who had introduced him had unwittingly taken his speech along with his introductory remarks back to his seat. No wonder the Secretary wanted to have his remarks in hand!

For me, as the boss's support structure, no two times were the same. There was often last-minute research that the boss wanted done. There were unexpected emergency calls that had to be taken and conveyed to the boss. There were unanticipated shifts in the pattern of activities we had expected.

In today's environment, it's a matter of monitoring for the boss what's going on in the world, in the industry, and in the community being visited. Things can happen, catastrophic things, unexpected things, from the time you leave home until the time you return from the trip. The job of the staff is to monitor news reports, which is easily done with a portable electronic device. I would even request that local newspapers be in the sedan that picked us up at the airport so that we could be current on local happenings.

Yes, the boss was always at a head table, sometimes elevated, sometimes just in the front of the room. It became habit for me to position myself in the room so that the boss could always see me. I would always let the boss know in advance where I would be so that he could make eye contact if he needed anything.

There was a memorable occasion in the summer of 1990 in Moscow. On the last night of a nine-day visit to the former Soviet Union, we Americans in the delegation and our Russian counterparts were guests of U.S. Ambassador Jack Matlock at his residence for the farewell dinner. Great food and seemingly endless vodka toasts.

Near the end of the evening General Powell, seated with his Soviet counterpart, General Mikhail Moiseyev, looked over, caught my eye, and head motioned for me to come over. I went over and bent down, and the chairman of the Joint Chiefs whispered that his Soviet counterpart was attempting to "drink him under the table." I asked him if he was up to the challenge, and the general responded, "I will never let it happen." It was a moment of trust and confidence when he needed to share something memorable with someone on the staff.

Yes, bosses are independent, and yes, many of them believe they need no help when traveling. Not so. Not only does the staff have the responsibility for support in advance of the trip, it has the responsibility for maintaining a presence during the trip to assist the boss in any way, expected or not.

Conversely, there are bosses who expect and need the support of staff members while traveling. It could be anything from personal care to professional advice. The staff, in keeping with the expression "Don't leave home without it," needs to be there in a support mode. Not an entourage, not more than is needed, but those required to keep the boss comfortable and assured that the day or night will go as expected.

18

Protect the Boss
from the Adoring

Not every boss is a public figure. Not every boss wants to be seen in public. But like it or not, there is a necessary public side to leaders who occupy positions of relevance or importance.

I have worked for people who were household names, people who were known and were expected to be seen and heard. One of them, Colin Powell, had rock-star status. We used to kiddingly say that we feared he was closing in too fast on Mother Teresa in popularity.

That may sound glamorous until you reach that point in the favorability polls. That's when you have to deal with the consequences.

It might be as simple as being surrounded when you enter a room, or it might be about being asked to pose for pictures. Or it might be a case of being asked to hold and kiss a baby. When those times come, it's less glamorous than one might think.

But when it comes with the territory and you inherit the responsibility to contend with it, you need to manage it. How do you do that? You do it responsibly. So as not to offend. So as not to annoy. So as not to disappoint.

I got a whiff of this air of popularity with several bosses I served, men of high distinction. At social gatherings or formal functions they would be surrounded quickly by the adoring. People who wanted time with the guest of honor. People who wanted a moment they could brag about the next day. People who wanted a picture taken for the scrapbook. It was hard to say no, but at the same time it had to be managed and controlled.

An example of doing that was making eye contact with the boss and seeing his signal that he had had enough. It was easy to tell him in front of the gathering that I needed a private moment with him. I was able to pull him away and find a quiet corner. We were able to decide when and where to reinsert ourselves into the social setting.

When military retirement came for Powell and me, the luxury of government sedans and airplanes disappeared. We were thrust into the life of the commoner: walking through airports, taking commercial jets, waiting for luggage. It was not uncommon to be run down by a caring citizen who would holler to us in an airport, "General Powell, General Powell. May I have your autograph? Can I take a picture of you?" Yes, we did care; yes, we did stop; yes, we did give them what they asked for. Why? It was a matter of showing our respect for them in return for their respect for him.

How interesting as the years passed that role reversal appeared in my life. Walking through security at my hometown airport in Syracuse, I glanced at the person in front of me. Handsome guy, looked familiar. I recognized none other than former NFL quarterback Doug Flutie. As he moved toward the gate, I turned to my assistant, Sue Virgil, who was behind me in line, and asked if she had spotted this once popular football star in front of us. She hadn't, so I gave her a clue about who it was. "Hail Mary pass?" The famous game-ending pass he threw for Boston College gave it away.

We reached our gate, and there he sat alone. He was waiting to board the same plane to Boston. I encouraged her to ask for his autograph. She went over to him, introduced herself, and asked if he would sign the cover of the program for the seminar we were about to conduct. Of all places, it was going to be held at Gillette

Stadium, home of the New England Patriots, for whom he once had played. With a huge smile he complied.

We had more time to kill before boarding the plane, so I asked if she had a camera. It just so happened she did. I encouraged her to ask him for an impromptu photo op. At first she didn't want to bother him again. Having had extensive experience in these kinds of situations, I told her no harm, no foul. However, she wanted a picture taken with him—not of him alone. I became the camera clicker and enjoyed capturing the moment.

He was as gracious as could be. She was as ecstatic as she could be. It was a Kodak moment for the adoring and the adored.

I have fumbled for more pens and taken more pictures than I care to recall to capture the moment for others. Each was as important as the one before it. With time I learned to manage them more efficiently. I learned how the general and I could gracefully exit the scene without offending anyone.

Flying commercially with General Powell became a challenge. By providing the designated air carrier advance notice, however, we typically were offered early boarding and seated in first class, front row left, behind the bulkhead, he next to the window and me on the aisle. The first time that happened, I thought it was very cool—that is, until the other passengers, who had seen us ushered aboard early, boarded the plane. There were awkward handshakes, autograph requests, even demands that he pose for a photo. In self-defense I learned quickly that a wide-open newspaper pointed toward the aisle served as good camouflage.

The adoring requests don't have to be this dramatic to be invasive. Someone may want private time with the boss. Someone may stop by unexpectedly. Someone may ask for that letter of reference that he or she needs that wasn't anticipated.

All these things take time, precious time, time that could be spent working down the list of priorities for the day. But you have to take time because all those people, all those requests, all those requirements are important and are part of being important. To deny them is insulting; to refuse them is inappropriate; to ignore them is worse.

Building a brand and building a reputation are part of what you should do for your boss. But with that comes dealing with the consequences of being popular. Being in demand requires skill and attention: skill at managing whatever it takes and attention to the details of doing it quickly and right.

Handling these requirements well comes with time. Anticipating the sorts of things that will be asked of your boss is intuitive. Knowing him or her well enough to minimize the time spent on the request is good management. Doing it in a way that is more a labor of love than necessity is caring. It pays off for the boss.

19

Anticipate the Boss's
Thinking and Decisions

There are numerous ways to determine what the boss is thinking or saying about what is happening in the life of the company. The most obvious approach to knowing is to ask him or her a relevant question. The next best is to be in the same room as the boss when that thinking comes to life so that you have a view from above.

Bearing witness to those words may come in the form of a one-on-one session, or the call to a staff meeting, or even a happenstance moment when you're in the same place as the boss. No matter how it happens, it's wise to pay attention to what's being said. If the meaning is unclear, definitely ask for further clarification.

Unless you're being told something in confidence, share the boss's thinking if asked or if it's helpful with others on the team. It helps if everyone knows the play that's been called so that a cause can be advanced successfully.

As I moved up in rank and position, such interactions were more commonplace. Always invited to the chairman of the Joint Chiefs' daily 8:30 a.m. meeting, I knew simply by listening and absorbing what was being planned, managed, or executed. This was most helpful in putting in context the answers to reporters' questions.

Never once did I cross the lines of classification, yet I didn't have to go running to the chairman for an answer to every one of the questions. Since there were dozens a day, that would have been a bit awkward and probably would have led to my getting fired.

Knowing my boss's thinking and decisions became especially important to me on February 9, 1993, around 7:30 p.m., when at home I received a call from a *New York Times* defense reporter. He asked if I'd comment on the rumor that General Powell planned to resign prematurely in anger over President Clinton's decision early in his presidency to allow gays and lesbians to join the military.

Not true, I told him. Having spoken to the chairman numerous times and having heard his view in many meetings, I knew he intended to work cooperatively with the executive branch, in particular the president, to resolve this question in the best interest of the armed forces of the United States. I knew too that he intended to serve out his term, which would normally end on September 30, 1993.

The reporter advised me that he had his information from three reliable sources. I told him that in the interest of his editors and readers he owed it to them to go back to his sources and not only question them about their views but tell them my response to those views. Two of those sources were out of the country, he said. My response was that the one available needed to be challenged.

I hung up the phone, drew a breath, and did a bit of work before hitting the sack around 10:00 p.m. It didn't take long for the phone to ring. At 10:30 p.m. a *Washington Post* reporter called to ask if there was any truth to the *New York Times* story, which had come out as part of the *New York Times* news service, an advance version released each night describing what would appear in print the next day. The phone rang incessantly until about 2:30 a.m., when I took the last call from Bernard Shaw of CNN. Dozens of reporters representing print, broadcast, and the wire services had called to ask the same thing: Was Powell retiring early over the gay issue? My answer to each was an emphatic "No!"

I knew the next day was not going to be an ordinary affair. I rose extra early and was at my desk in the Pentagon at 5:45 a.m. Sure enough, in the February 10 first edition of the *New York*

Times there appeared on the front page, above the fold, a story with the headline that screamed out, "Joint Chiefs' Head Is Said to Request Early Retirement."

After reading the story, I called the chairman at his home and explained what had occurred. I told him I would send a copy of the newspaper with his driver who was going to pick him up at his quarters around 6:30 a.m. He said we would discuss it when he arrived.

A bell tolled mindfully in my brain. I asked one of my deputies to go out to the front steps of the Pentagon to see if anyone was lurking in the cool, early morning darkness. The navy commander I had dispatched returned breathlessly in a few minutes to tell me that a CBS reporter and cameraman were awaiting the chairman's arrival.

Another call was made to the chairman to tell him what to expect when he drove up to the Pentagon's River Entrance, which was his custom. "We need to take this head on," I told him. "Stop and tell the reporter the truth." Upon arrival, he did that at the top of the steps.

I asked if he was ready to do more of the same. He nodded yes. I hustled down the corridor to the small designated rooms where reporters from ABC and NBC were getting ready to tell this breaking news story to their television audiences. I asked if they would like to talk to the chairman in person. But of course, was their answer. General Powell visited them within the half hour and did remote interviews for the *Today Show* and *Good Morning America*. Later that morning we went over to the CNN studios in Washington, where he sat down with Bernard Shaw for an interview.

In the business, they call it a grand slam when you do all the networks. We had effectively killed the story in one fell swoop. The story died, normalcy was restored, and the reporter paid a penalty for getting it wrong. He was temporarily removed from the defense beat.

If I hadn't known the chairman's intentions, I might have gotten this wrong. An incendiary story like this could have razed the

Washington forest. It also could have burned a bridge to the White House. We had enough going on in life in normal circumstances not to need extra drama. I was also fortunate to have in place the trust factor that is so important between superior and subordinate. Just another day in paradise.

20

Think Beyond the Horizon

I have had a lot of people work for me over the course of time. They have been very busy men and women. I know that because typically I gave them lots to do. These were people in the public sector as well as those in not-for-profit and for-profit organizations. They were the kinds of work environments where you didn't have time to watch the clock and the day slipped by before you could get everything done. You stayed busy but had a great sense of accomplishment at the end of the day.

Having grown up in the army, I was taught well that you need to prepare not just for the inevitable but for the unexpected. That's why there are war plans before there are wars. It was ingrained in me to think strategically about most things. You don't necessarily need to have been in the military to think this way, but if it becomes part of your DNA, you will be better prepared for most things in your personal and professional lives.

If your boss doesn't tell you that you have some responsibility to think beyond the moment, or as I call it, look beyond the horizon for potential destinations, you need to do that for the boss. You should be asking what organizational interests are at stake for what lies ahead. What is the purpose and what proposed actions need to be taken to achieve those interests? What costs are involved? What resources are needed? What is the desired outcome? You should be making an honest appraisal of the landscape as it exists today but also of how it is likely to look tomorrow.

One way to do these things is to have a strategic management process. That consists of strategic thinking and strategic planning. They are not one and the same, but they are both essential in any thoughtful strategy-making process.

Strategic thinking comes first and is done by connecting the past, the present, and the future in ways that allow for creativity and the invention of ideas, the what-ifs of life, if you will.

Strategic planning converts these ideas into programmatic actions built on analysis and designed intent: the then-whats of life. For the boss, this could make an important contribution to a grand strategy, which is a collection of plans and policies to advance the organization's interests.

There are ample examples of unexpected or unpleasant things that can happen in any organizational life: a financial downturn, a necessary layoff, a product recall, a malevolent act. Any of these things could happen at any point in time. If trends start to develop or hints of crisis surface, you need to be prepared. It's too late if the doors blow off at 2 p.m. and you aren't ready to respond.

Many of the routine staff meetings you have should end up being brainstorming sessions in anticipation of or in response to events that occur. When the boss goes around the table asking questions or wanting suggestions, it's a cerebral moment for which you need and want to be prepared. If you are a regular victim of those dreaded staff meetings, come armed. Have at your fingertips well-reasoned, thoughtful advice for the boss or any other person at the table who seeks it.

For me the world of strategic thinking and planning came alive in January 1997 when Colin Powell agreed to chair a summit in Philadelphia. It was called the Presidents' Summit for America's Future. All living presidents and first ladies with the exception of President Reagan, who was unable to attend because of health issues, were in attendance. Convened in Philadelphia that April, the summit was designed to draw attention to the some 15 million "at-risk youth in America." An astronomical number! Something needed to be done. The summit assembled members of Congress, governors, corporate and not-for-profit executives, religious leaders, educators, and philanthropists. It drew the attention of 1,400 reporters, not just from the United States but from around the world, who covered the event.

The attendees met for three days and discussed among themselves how they could help: what they should do and how they could do it. Powell agreed to chair an organization that was the outgrowth of this seminal event, and all seemed fine until the general and I returned to our offices in Virginia after the summit. He asked me, "What do we do now, Smullen?" There was no blueprint or model or example of what to do and how to do it. As his chief of staff, my goal was to help raise some money, hire a staff, build out some office space, and develop a strategic plan. It was by far the most challenging but most exciting opportunity one could ask for.

We created an organization from whole cloth. We called it America's Promise—The Alliance for Youth. We found ways to bring resources into the lives of young Americans: a healthy start, a safe space, mentoring relationships, educational components, and volunteer opportunities for kids. Damned if it didn't work. We got tons of help from companies such as Allstate Insurance, whose 53,000 employees at the time were asked to volunteer and become involved in the lives of youth. They did just that and made a difference by becoming coaches, tutors, mentors, and caring adults in as many ways as possible.

Did this take strategic thinking and strategic planning? Of course. Was it without difficulty? Of course not. But we moved the needle when it came to taking kids off the at-risk road of life and putting them on the successful highways of life.

I didn't get day-to-day guidance from the boss, but I gave him day-to-day progress reports. As chairman, General Powell used to call himself the Johnny Appleseed of America's Promise, and I came to think of myself as a planter of many of those seeds.

21

Build and Maintain
the Boss's Credibility

Serving the boss well is more than about making that person happy or even keeping him or her satisfied. It does, however, have a lot to do with building and maintaining the boss's credibility.

Credibility means different things to different people. My criterion for credibility is whether a person can be trusted, can be believed, can be taken at his or her word. That is important whether it's by an outsider or by someone on the staff. You can help build such credibility for your boss.

As is the case for the boss, maintaining credibility is important for you, too. You are a reflection of that person. As your credibility grows, so will the degree to which you're sought after as an informative, thoughtful source of well-reasoned advice that you can lend the boss.

If the boss's credibility is intact, people within the organization will follow that leader. If either you or the boss loses that all-important credibility, you might as well fold up your tent and go home. The road ahead will be lined with mishaps.

You can pick up the newspaper any day and find examples of people who have lost their way: corporate leaders, politicians, people in any walk of life who forget who they are and where they are going. Lying, cheating, and stealing aren't just examples of breaking the law; they're about breaking a bond with people who trusted them, who believed in them, who followed them because they thought they were headed in the right direction.

Some of those people who err go to jail; others step down from elected office. Not just guilty as charged or sentenced as deemed fit but forever embarrassed. Unfortunately, the shame is not confined to them. It affects their families, their friends, and their organizational following.

One of the most egregious examples of corporate misconduct was the Enron debacle that began in 2001. Kenneth Lay was the CEO of Enron, one of the world's largest electricity and natural gas traders. The company was based in Houston, Texas. Lay was one of that city's biggest philanthropists. His reputation and his credibility were solid, especially among the Enron employees, whom he encouraged to add to their 401(k) plans by buying Enron stock.

Unfortunately for them and for Lay, the Enron house of cards started to collapse when a whistle-blower caused the Securities and Exchange Commission to launch a formal investigation into possible conflict of interest related to the company's overrated earnings. Lay and other corporate leaders at Enron were engaged in a plot to inflate profit and hide losses. He resigned in disgrace and was forced to testify before Congress. Indicted in 2004, he stood trial and was found guilty. Before his sentencing in 2006, Lay died of a heart attack. Meanwhile, the company went bankrupt and all those employees' savings were lost along with a lot of credibility.

Someone should have been monitoring the actions of Enron's leadership. If you are responsible for that type of oversight and for the boss's credibility and reputation, what is your standard of conduct acceptability and mission accomplishment? If you don't have one, get one.

In what form? One may be simply profit or loss numbers, and another may be retention levels. It could come in the form of feedback solicited from stakeholders, starting with the employees. There's nothing unusual about conducting surveys, nothing difficult about having town hall meetings, nothing complex about creating a chat room on your website. They are means that will tell you how the boss is doing or how the organization is faring.

If you are a handler for the boss and don't see or sense an established standard coming from your leader, it's time for a chat with that person. Ask for a verbal description of the desired standard or create one yourself. Put it in writing, get it blessed, distribute it to all the parties concerned. If you get pushback or resistance, stand your ground. This is not about you, and it is not just about the boss either; it is about everyone who chooses to follow that person.

Almost every organization has a code of conduct, a set of ethics or rules of the road. At least it should. That doesn't guarantee that anybody reads them, follows them, or cares about them. When was the last time you looked at the state of your organizational standards? When was the last time you sat the staff down for a "conscience" session? If you have a meeting designed for that purpose, don't be asking and answering your own questions. If you believe in feedback and you believe in honesty from others, you believe in progress.

I have worked for bosses who lacked credibility. I wished more than anything that they would be replaced. That's not always how the system works. Their lack of credibility affected all of us in ways that made the job more difficult to do. Discussions with those bosses to help them restore their credibility fell on deaf ears. Choices were few: quit, endure, or plug away at change.

Actually, the bottom-up approach is not the best or easiest way to fix a problem, but it may be all you have. My tactic was to motivate the staff and keep the boss in balance; it was not a perfect approach, but it was the best I had available at the time. Fortunately, in each case, those bosses were gone before I was and their successors were better models. Time heals all wounds. In those difficult cases, the advancement in time brought new faces, and they took us to new places.

As I place credibility on the hierarchy of character traits, it looms at the top. It's more than a word, it's more than a wish, it's everything. You bruise it, you lose it. To not lose it, protect it for all it's worth; it's golden.

Credibility is not something you are born with. It's something you earn and build over time. You can't put it on your résumé, but you need to put it into practice, for every day and in virtually every way that credibility will be tested. Stand up to that test and pass it with flying colors. You will not regret it. In fact, you will come to treasure it.

22

Be a Gatekeeper, Not a Gate Blocker

The more powerful one gets, the more protective one can become. Of what? Of time, of territory, of the world one manages for the boss or for oneself. Such instincts may feel good for the moment, but over time they can be obstructive.

Stakeholders looking at what you do and how you do it may see you as a legitimate gatekeeper who provides access to people, places, and things or a gate blocker who uses barriers and excuses as obstacles to progress. Arrogance and self-serving resistance to providing assistance to both insiders and outsiders can create a toxic workplace environment where people fear to tread.

I've been fortunate to work for bosses who may not necessarily have kept their door open every moment but were approachable if you knocked on their door. That promotes a healthy organizational climate. It also carries over to subordinates. In my case, unless I was having a private conversation with a staff member or visitor, my door was always open to others.

One day, not long after the first Gulf War in 1991, there was a knock on my open Pentagon office door. Standing there with a big smile on his face was an army sergeant who had been the enlisted driver for my former boss, Admiral Bill Crowe. I hadn't seen Sergeant First Class Michael Rodriguez since the admiral retired as chairman of the Joint Chiefs in September 1989. Mike had gone on to drive for people in the White House.

"Sir, do you have a second?" he asked. Mike told me he needed a favor and felt comfortable asking me. The "why me?" wasn't clear, but I nodded and listened. He told me his uncle owned a fish market in the Boston area. Moreover, the now late General Norman Schwarzkopf was his hero for having achieved victory on the battlefield against the Iraqi army in Operation Desert Storm earlier that year. So far, I was happy for his uncle and for Stormin' Norman, as the general was known.

Then came the ask. "In gratitude my uncle wants to send General Schwarzkopf a lobster," Mike said. "In Saudi Arabia or when he gets home?" I asked. "Right now, while he's in Riyadh," Mike said. "And I know," he went on, "that if anyone can get it to him it's you."

Nice of you to think so, I thought. I'm not even a fan of H. Norman Schwarzkopf, Jr., and I don't do magic. However, I was intrigued with the notional challenge of getting a live crustacean to the table of the Central Command commander some 8,000 miles away before the lobster expired.

"Promise nothing to your uncle," I told Mike, "but I'll see what I can do." After he left, I asked myself: Legal? Yes. Moral? Yes. Fattening? Yes. Worth it? Yes, but not without considerable coordination and a dose of luck.

This movement had a lot of moving parts, literally and figuratively. Between a thousand other things going on in my life, I picked away at gathering information. Did the general even like lobster, and if he got one, would he eat it? Yes, came the curious answer from Saudi Arabia. What military air base was closest to Boston and flying cargo to that theater? Hanscom Air Force Base in Bedford, Massachusetts, some 20 miles outside of Boston. How long could a lobster survive in dry ice and seaweed? Up to a week give or take if packed well. How big would the lobster be, oh, by the way? Most likely 24 to 26 pounds came the answer. This translated to an elderly lobster, some 75 to 100 years of age.

The key to success was the receptivity to the idea by the staff at Hanscom. Starting at the top, I called the base commander's office and asked for his chief of staff. Could he, would he? Several calls and weeks later the answer came. If you can get the precious cargo to the flight line by 9:00 a.m. on Sunday, there is a flight going to Riyadh with a stop in Rota, Spain, to refuel.

The next call was to Mike Rodriguez. Can your uncle deliver the designated cargo on time to Hanscom? For sure, was his answer. Last call to Riyadh. Can someone retrieve the cargo and get it to the general's orderly to put it in a large kettle, boil it, and put it on the table? Table is set, they said.

After several calls with the folks at Hanscom and those in Riyadh the next Wednesday, I was assured the lobster had made it. Long, tough journey for the old boy.

My satisfaction lay in having successfully been a gatekeeper who had opened some doors for three people. Nothing further was required, but it came in the form of a reward the next Friday night. Sitting outside the front door of my home, on the stoop, was an unmarked cardboard box. Cautiously I opened it to find a large live lobster and a note from Mike Rodriguez saying, "My uncle thanks you."

The English poet Alexander Pope captured it best when he wrote, "Blessed is the man who expects nothing, for he shall never be disappointed." Actually, as someone who was born in Boston but moved to Maine at age 15, I was delighted with the seafood blessing.

If you are a traffic cop for your boss, you control many things: access or not, the color of the lights—red or green—and the atmospherics that accompany who goes where and who sees whom. Of course, you should validate the need. Ask the right questions and set the limits of time and the takeaway.

When I retired with Colin Powell in 1993, I started as a staff of one person who took the calls, controlled the calendar, and set the limits of access. Less powerful in my mind than purposive. Ask the right questions: what and why? If the reason was weak, the response was a polite "Right now the schedule won't permit." Never was the boss the reason for the rejection; better the calendar or the clock.

Before a visit or phone call made it onto the calendar, I would clear it with the boss, accompanied by a recommendation of why or why not to consent to the meeting or phone call. Scrupulousness was the gauge, and merit was the metric.

Never block access to the throne because you have the power to do so; give or deny access to it because it's the right thing or not. If you find yourself someday knocking on a door and not being answered, you will better understand that power can be corrosive and ultimate power can be ultimately destructive if it is not managed wisely.

23

Don't Speak for the Boss Unless He Asks or Knows

Everyone has an ego—small, medium, or large. It's the large ones that tend to get in the way of good sense. They exceed their boundaries, and when they do that, they don't play well to the masses. This can become particularly problematic when a "full of himself" subordinate develops an air of importance that goes over the top.

That can happen in the workplace if the boss fails to place limits on those who have decision-making responsibilities on his or her behalf. It can also happen if the junior in rank simply chooses to ignore what he or she is told or is expected to do. Who loses? The boss does if he or she hasn't checked what's being said or done. The organization loses because the lack of constraints or controls can cost money, image, or reputation.

When actions go beyond the limits of guidance, they can be seen or caught if there's a system for diagnosis or evaluation. If it's a matter of words rather than deeds, that's more difficult to diagnose or detect unless it's a front-page story that catches one's eye.

You may be able to get away with having misspoken if it's at the local level and it appears in print only once if at all. At the state level, if you are out ahead of the boss with your statement, the story may last a day or two. At the national level, the attention drawn and the stir created can cause havoc for a good stretch of time.

We had just returned from the first of several trips to Saudi Arabia in the wake of Saddam Hussein's invasion of Kuwait on August 2, 1990. His army, the world's sixth largest at the time, had easily occupied neighboring Kuwait, and President George H. W. Bush took exception. He offered to come to the aid of a U.S. ally and its people. The United States asked the royal family if we could station U.S. military personnel in their kingdom, which borders Kuwait and Iraq. They agreed, and we had just visited the first wave of troops stationed in that country.

On the morning after our return, which was Sunday, September 16, 1990, I strolled to my driveway to get the morning paper. It was warm and sunny; it felt nice to be home. That is, until I unfolded my copy of the *Washington Post* and stopped dead in my tracks. There on the front page was a story describing remarks by the U.S. Air Force chief of staff, General Michael J. Dugan, to reporters on extensive flights aboard a dedicated U.S. Air Force plane to and from Saudi Arabia the week before.

According to the article, he had revealed to the journalists accompanying him on the trip that the Iraqi air force had very little capability and that its army was incompetent. Furthermore, he announced that the U.S. military had plans "to bomb Baghdad relentlessly and 'decapitate' the Iraqi leadership by targeting Hussein personally, along with his family, his senior leaders, his palace guard and even his mistress."

No sooner had I finished reading the piece than my home phone rang. "Did you see the *Post* piece on Dugan?" asked my boss. "Yes, sir," I replied. "What did you think?" asked General Colin L. Powell, chairman of the Joint Chiefs. "I think he got out in front of his headlights," was my response.

"Call your buddies in the air force and ask them how and why this happened," he directed. It took only one phone call to get the answer. An air force officer who had been on the trip with Dugan said his boss had sat for considerable time with reporters from the *Post*, the *Los Angeles Times*, and *Aviation Week & Space*

Technology. Five other air force generals on the trip also participated in the "far too long" interviews on both legs of the trip.

"What was he thinking?" I asked. My colleague did not attempt to defend his boss. Sounding dismayed, he said aides to the secretary of defense had discouraged the air force chief from taking reporters along. He personally had warned his chief against speaking to them for so long. Both to no avail.

When I called General Powell back with what I had learned, he asked me to find out where Dugan was at that moment because he wanted to speak with him. He also revealed that Secretary of Defense Dick Cheney was none too happy with the "loose-lipped" account of things said.

My air force source told me his boss was in Florida visiting a military unit. When I conveyed that to the chairman, he told me the secretary was taking a walk along the canal in Washington, D.C., to sort this out. Cheney's pondering jaunt didn't seem like a particularly good sign to me.

The next morning around 7:45 the chairman summoned me to his office to advise me that Cheney had consulted with President Bush and that they had concluded that General Dugan had shown "poor judgment at a very sensitive time." General Powell then told me that at 8 a.m. that day the secretary intended to fire Dugan.

He would not be the first top general in history to be dismissed, but it was still a big deal. President Truman had ousted General Douglas A. MacArthur in 1951, but in more contemporary times it was unprecedented. Yet this simply was another time and another moment when national-security considerations trumped bravado.

For me the lessons were many. Certainly know where your position is in the proverbial chain of command. Know what you can and should say about issues of high importance, in this case a war plan that had the highest degree of classification in military circles. Think about the consequences of what you're saying, who you're saying it to, and who ultimately will hear your words and decide their impact.

Yes, there was ego involved. Yes, General Dugan had been exhilarated by what he saw when he visited troops and facilities in Saudi Arabia. But to speak on behalf of what amounted to the national command authority was a bridge too far. He hadn't been asked to do so; in fact, he had been discouraged from doing what he did. He didn't even have the sense or courtesy to tell his many bosses—the secretary of the Air Force, the chairman of the Joint Chiefs, the secretary of defense, and the president—what he either intended to do or had done.

In times like these, and there will be times like these at every level and in every sector, there needs to be a standard of judgment that stands above jurisdiction. Author Andrew J. Holmes provided such a yardstick when he said, "It is well to remember that the entire population of the universe, with one trifling exception, is composed of others."

Yes, strive to achieve positions of importance and influence as best you can in your professional life. But remember that you are only one person on the road of life and you needn't run over people with who you are and what you believe.

24

Push the Boss out in Public
When There Is a Purpose

The art of storytelling has historical roots that go back centuries. The earliest forms of storytelling were primarily verbal expressions combined with gestures. It is an art form that lives today and relates to the practical and purposeful use of the narrative.

From a business standpoint it is essential to tell your story. It is used to interpret the past or present and shape the future. It is used to manage conflict and to resolve difficult issues facing an organization. It plays an important role in the reasoning process.

Taught today in university classrooms, storytelling prepares young people for what lies ahead in the marketplace of ideas. For a professional in today's world, storytelling is an incredibly important tool that must be learned and practiced.

As a communicator, telling my organization's story was second nature for me. However, for some people I advised that was not always the case.

I recall being assigned as a public affairs advisor to the secretary of the army and the army chief of staff, the senior civilian and uniformed officials, respectively, of my service. My position had been created because neither was very active in telling the army's story and they needed a push. I began asking them to give speeches and engage in press interviews to tell stakeholders about the issues of the day.

To create a comfort zone for them, I decided to develop what I called an Issues Book. Seeking the help of a three-star general, the director of the army staff, I drafted a memorandum that he signed and that then went out to the entire army staff. Essentially it directed subject-matter experts to create one-page papers describing various issues that were or could potentially be in the news. That included operational matters, types of equipment being tested, personnel issues, and legal affairs: hot-button topics of the day. With the staff's help I kept the Issues Book current.

For the secretary and the chief of staff, this book became like a Linus blanket. I would routinely update the contents in advance of every event I proposed. I made sure they had it in hand the Friday before the designated activity, whether it was a speech or a press interview, so that they had the weekend to review the contents. They came to expect it, and it served as a form of encouragement to do more.

Because not all news is good news, they were prepared for any issue, positive or negative. In fact, with large organizations or institutions lots can go wrong. Army General John Vessey, former chairman of the Joint Chiefs of Staff, used to say that with as many people as there are in the armed forces of the United States, somewhere and at any point in time someone was acting improperly or something bad could be happening.

Rather than hiding from such things, leaders must step up to the plate and admit wrongdoing or malfunction. It's not cause for embarrassment as much as it is an indication of the need for a full-disclosure admission. The adage "bad news does not get any better with age" is surely true. However, if the story is positive, even spectacular, shout it from the rafters. It not only builds the brand, it is simply good for business.

Not all bosses are going to buy into this philosophy. In fact, the twelfth chairman of the Joint Chiefs of Staff, General Colin Powell, wanted nothing to do with all my proposals to be the public face and voice of the armed forces when he first assumed the position. I continued to ask him to participate in public events;

he continued to decline the offers. It was an extremely frustrating period for me. A cautious man, the general was simply getting his sea legs as the senior uniformed officer in the U.S. Armed Forces. Finally, two months after he took office, he accepted an invitation to speak at Kansas State University. It went extremely well. His confidence level rose; my spirits soared.

Success begets success, but it doesn't come without the support required. If I ever asked the chairman to commit to something publicly, I would always provide him information on the event, the personalities involved, the audience he would be speaking to, and the desired story line. If it was a speech that had a Q and A session afterward, I would provide possible questions related to the subject. If it was an interview with a reporter, I would provide him not just anticipated questions but proposed answers. Preparation on my part and familiarity on his part was the order of the day.

I was very fortunate that over time the more I asked of him, the more he did. I kept the numbers during his four years as chairman. From October 1989 until September 1993, he participated in 408 public events. They included congressional hearings, speeches before public forums, and talks to visiting groups. In the case of press events, there were 257 occasions when he engaged with the media. These included press conferences, media availabilities, and one-on-one interviews. In the aggregate, 665 times he told the story of the Armed Forces of the United States to various stakeholders.

You may not have the luxury of having a Colin Powell as your boss, and that's fine. That doesn't mean your boss shouldn't be out in public telling the organization's story or speaking on behalf of the organization. If you want your brand to shine, you need to polish it by putting the boss out in public when there is a purpose.

25

Prepare the Boss for Each Event or Activity

You should want a feeling of confidence in whatever you do. You should want to feel competent in whatever way you do it. You should want your boss to feel the same ways about himself or herself.

One way to do that is to support the boss in all that he or she must accomplish. That takes more than mere chance or a bit of luck. It requires preparing the boss in everything he or she does along the way.

It helps to know the boss and his or her likes, dislikes, interests, and expectations. Gain the boss's confidence in what you can do to achieve those things. Clarify mutual expectations early.

If the boss is new to you or you are new to him or her, have a conversation to get to know the boss better. Put the boss's needs at the center of your universe.

As in the Boy Scout motto "Be prepared," get ready to support any event in which the boss agrees to participate. Gather information. Not only the five Ws (who, what, when, where, why) but the how of turning it into a successful venture as well.

Ask a lot of questions and accrue a lot of answers. Put them in writing and stand by for a conversation that will provide more detail as necessary. Anticipate everything.

If it's a speech, for example, ask not just about the size of audience but about its demographic composition as well. If the requester hasn't asked for a particular subject for the talk, what might the audience want to know about? What's the layout of the room? Is there a podium? Does it have a light on it so the boss can see the speech? Does it have a lip and a slant so the boss can read it without holding the text or see it clearly when looking down with glasses on? Who is introducing your boss? What's the length of time he or she will have? How much time will the boss have for questions?

Perhaps most important of all is the sound. Is it a podium microphone, or is it a lavalier microphone? In either case, remember that the microphone may be live, and if the boss is overheard saying something he or she doesn't want others to hear, that may cause great embarrassment for the guest of honor.

Overhead lighting is another consideration. Too bright or too hot can be deadly when it is shone on the speaker. Overhead stage lighting can affect the visibility of a PowerPoint presentation by washing it out. Lighting in the room should be high enough for the faces in the audience to be seen by the speaker.

When it comes to technology, there are certain things to know in advance. If a PowerPoint presentation is going to be used, compatibility is critical. If the organization asks for visuals in advance, a determination must be made whether you want to share that intellectual property. If so, ask that it not be shared in advance.

Where is the screen in relationship to the podium? If an assistant will operate the PowerPoint, where will he or she be in relationship to the speaker? In some cases, flash drives are not permitted; if they are not, you may need to use a CD-ROM. It's always helpful to have a technician standing by should a need occur.

When it comes to video teleconferences and Skyping, both popular and useful for long-distance venues, know how to do it in advance on both ends. Run a pretest far in advance and just before the event as well.

Writing support for a speech the boss will give is an art form. Providing the speechwriter guidance is essential: everything from the purpose to the punch line. Write in the voice of the boss. Think of it as the boss having a conversation with the audience.

What points does the boss want to make, and what does he or she want the audience to remember? That conversation should occur at least one month in advance with the boss if at all possible. When should the boss get the first draft? A good rule of thumb is two weeks in advance. Why? To gain familiarity with it, to grow comfortable with it, to make changes to it, and to rehearse it. A speech may go through as many as six drafts, and changes may be made up until the last minute. Assume there's no such thing as it being too perfect.

As someone who prides himself on attention to detail, I worked hard helping Colin Powell give one of the most important speeches of his public life until that point in time. Asked to give a keynote address at the 1996 Republican National Convention in San Diego, he worked diligently on the text and the messaging. He war-gamed it with me and made changes right up to the end. The end, I thought was on Saturday, August 11, when he put it to bed and went home.

For me, it was a late night at the office. Putting the words into the right font and setting the width of margins and paginating it so that every page ended with a period were all important details.

Feeling very smug when it was done, I confidently placed it in his speech box, turned off the lights, and headed home about 10:00 p.m. with the box in hand. The next morning I met him at the executive air terminal at Reagan Airport in Washington, D.C. We boarded an executive jet, courtesy of a campaign supporter, and headed for the West Coast.

With a book in hand I settled comfortably in the forward compartment ready to read myself to sleep flying across the country. My boss was in the rear compartment with the plane's owner, locked in conversation. We had no sooner leveled off when he came forward with speech in hand, sat down next to me, and asked, "Are you ready to go to work?" "I beg your pardon, sir," I said. He announced, "I want to make some changes to this speech."

My heart skipped a beat. I had sent the text to a staffer in San Diego the night before so that it could be uploaded into a teleprompter for a two-hour-long rehearsal session scheduled at the San Diego Convention Center soon after we were to land.

A hostage at 36,000 feet, I knew I had a problem. Whatever changes we made would have to be transferred to the teleprompter script upon landing. That would take some time; we would never be ready for the rehearsal in time. I called ahead and asked for forgiveness and some divine intervention. That came in the form of Senator Kay Bailey Hutchison agreeing to trade rehearsal times, she before he.

Upon landing, we headed for the convention center with just enough time to make the changes with the help of the teleprompter technician. When our rehearsal time arrived, we were ready, a bit breathless but prepared for a prime-time rehearsal.

The true prime time came the next night when the general followed former president Gerald Ford and former president George H. W. Bush with his remarks. Former first lady Nancy Reagan followed.

It was a magical moment for the general, and it was a scary moment for me. Had we not asked the teleprompter operator we had for the rehearsal to run it Monday night for us, the timing might not have been as perfect as it was. When it was over, I let out a sigh of relief, like air out of a punctured tire. The audience would never know what had gone into the talk. They loved it.

Anticipation works most of the time. Support must occur all the time. Take responsibility for the good and the bad, for the known and the unknown, for the intended and unintended consequences of everything you do for the boss.

Each situation is going to be different. Keep a notebook of lessons learned. Cross-train the members of your team. Make sure the team learns from these experiences.

Each boss is different. You must come to know your boss's work style. Aim for early wins in important areas. Gain the boss's confidence.

The term *intervention* has many meanings. Generally, it refers to involving oneself in a situation to alter an action or development. It is the involvement, participation, and engagement in the activities of another. It is the act of sharing.

As you provide support to your boss, take care to improve the situation, whatever it may be, for him or her. You'll be glad you did. The boss will be grateful you did.

26

Resolve Conflict for the Boss

Most people would prefer not to argue or fight with someone, especially in the workplace. It's not private, it's not pretty, and it certainly is not conducive to a positive office atmosphere.

If we do bring bad moods or manners to the office, we could use a little counseling, for we're not being helpful to those around us who want, expect, and deserve a work environment that is healthy, even happy.

Conflict resolution is both an art and a science. A subject taught at universities and practiced by diplomats on the world stage, conflict management is used to help people understand better why other people do certain things. Whether at the international level, at the corporate level, or on an individual basis, there are certain commonalities that come into play.

A starting point is to look at the histories of those in conflict. The personalities involved are another factor. What have been their past and more recent actions toward the adversary? What are their goals and objectives for engaging in conflict to begin with? What is the desired end state of those in disagreement?

In the workplace, assuming you have management responsibility over others, you are in a position and have a need to resolve differences among employees who are at odds. If you have supervisory responsibility but not ultimate responsibility, do not assume that the boss can or will get involved in resolving disputes. I've worked

for bosses who want no part in dealing with conflict between subordinates. They expect others to solve the problem no matter how
small or how large. Having somebody else fix it is their expectation; it may even be their directive.

A good place to start if that requirement falls on you is to look
at the differences and the obstacles to be overcome. Consider the
options, stake out the solutions, and get after the problem. When
there's a lot at stake for the boss or for a project important to him
or her, the urgency to find the right answer to a problem involving
conflict is high.

When the writing and editing of Colin Powell's memoirs was
complete in the summer of 1995, focus shifted to promotion of
his 613-page book. I scheduled dozens of print interviews, all of
which were embargoed until the scheduled release of the book on
Friday, September 15, 1995.

Random House demanded that there be a cloak of secrecy leading up to the formal release and first book signing the next day in
McLean, Virginia. Their goal was to distribute 950,000 copies, the
first printing, to bookstores across the country.

Leading up to that date, there were other scheduled events:
an excerpt in *TIME* magazine on Monday, September 11, and
an ABC *20/20* interview with Barbara Walters that Friday night,
September 15.

The *20/20* feature was the centerpiece, and ABC invested heavily in it. The general and I traveled to Jamaica in August for a
series of interviews with Barbara Walters in the country where his
parents had been born. The visit to those family roots was coupled
with a stop at Fort Benning, Georgia, where Powell as a lieutenant
had planted his military roots. Barbara interviewed him several
times in both places. Later, we met and he walked with her in his
old South Bronx neighborhood called Banana Kelly. Lots of time
and money on ABC's part went into this production.

Then the roof caved in on the carefully orchestrated publicity
plan when *Newsweek* sabotaged it by somehow obtaining a bootleg
copy and releasing its own unauthorized excerpt on September 4, a

week before the *TIME* cover story was to run and 11 days before the Walters piece was to air.

We flew to New York City on Tuesday, September 5, for a Random House–hosted book party at the ritzy I Trulli restaurant in midtown. No sooner had I walked through the door with Powell to join the company of the rich and famous who had been invited than I was attacked verbally by Ms. Walters, who was not at all happy with *Newsweek*'s hijacking of the story. Anger and frustration were in her voice. "How could you let this happen?" she asked. "What am I to do now that I have been preempted?"

I asked her if we could retire to a corner for a more private discussion. *TIME* editor Jim Kelly joined us. He was none too happy either about having been walloped by the competition notwithstanding the routine existence of this ancient journalistic tradition called scooping.

Conflict at its best, or in this case at its worst for us. I asked for the chance to continue this heated discussion in a more civil way after dinner. They agreed to give me time to inform the boss of the problem before we sat down for dinner.

After the meal and the praise heaped on Harold Evans, the publisher, and the author, the crowd dispersed. Evans, Walters, Kelly, the general, and I found that proverbial quiet little table in the corner for a not so quiet conversation on how to salvage the situation. *Newsweek* had beaten everyone to the punch. Our goal was to snatch victory from the jaws of defeat.

We sought something quite useful in resolving conflict. It's called compromise. In this case, we agreed to two things: that *20/20* could air their special on Powell earlier than planned and that we would conduct an additional interview with *TIME* to add to their cover story of the following week.

We met the next morning in my room at the Trump Tower with *TIME* writers John Stacks and Michael Kramer. They even brought a photographer who rearranged the furniture to provide the proper backdrop for the Powell sidebar interview, which was as much about his political aspirations as it was about the book.

For a couple of old soldiers unaccustomed to show biz, it was something to behold.

We had both experienced plenty of conflict in our careers on the battlefield and in conference rooms where talks were tense, but this conflict took the cake. We felt we had barely escaped the wrath of two journalists who were hopping mad at us for a situation we did not create. Nevertheless, we needed to solve the issue so that their dignity and reputations were salvaged.

Actually, all the additional publicity provided courtesy of *Newsweek*'s cover story added to the attention surrounding the book and the author. It also contributed to speculation about his political intentions. *My American Journey* was so popular and successful that it had multiple printings and was published in many languages over time.

If there is a moral regarding conflict in the workplace, it's to face up to it, attack it quickly, and resolve it properly and permanently. Allowing it to persist will only make matters worse. If the boss doesn't want to deal with conflict in the organization or on his or her staff, so be it. The boss is the boss!

You, however, out of loyalty to that boss and a duty to serve that boss well must take action. The boss need not know you had to do it or even how well you did it as long as it was done in a way that put the conflict behind you. That is far better than what previously stood before you.

27

Help Manage Risk

When you sense that things could go wrong, you can lock the door and pray or you can do something to prevent the bad omen from coming true. Better yet, you can engage in risk management.

It isn't difficult, and it's especially smart. It's a process by which you identify, assess, and prioritize the uncertainties that lie before you so that you can control the probability of occurrence of unfortunate events. Risk management is the proactive approach to eliminating or minimizing risks. You may not have the power to avoid or control risk, but you can manage and cope with the likelihood of it occurring.

Risks abound in the business world. They range from financial setbacks, accidents, project failure, and product malfunction to cyberthreats, computer viruses, social media attacks, and legal liability. The impact of any of these things can be devastating to an organization.

Risk management has incredible value. It should be an integral part of doing business. It should be part of staff meeting discussions and the strategic thinking that the boss needs so that he or she can make decisions that avoid problems for the organization.

Any unwanted event can endanger the ability to satisfy an objective or achieve success within an organization. Not every organization can afford to hire or have a risk officer, but any organization can have senior representatives who are thinking aggressively about what lies ahead that could be problematic and can help the boss with built-in risk control and containment measures. If this is done well, an organization can avoid risks altogether.

On a beautiful September morning in 2001, I learned the hard way that risk is everywhere. As the chief of staff of the State Department, I was returning from the morning staff meeting when a junior staffer alerted me that a plane had just flown into the World Trade Center in New York City. I rushed to my office, turned on the television, and watched another plane fly into the second tower. Not long afterward, I glanced out of my seventh-floor office window and saw the building I had worked in for 10 years, the Pentagon, on fire. By that time it was clear that this was a devastating event of enormous proportions.

I went with the deputy secretary of state, Richard Armitage, to the State Department Command Center. In a secure room we were connected by a video teleconference with representatives of the White House, the CIA, the FBI, the National Security Council, and other key agencies. Collectively, we concluded that the nation was under attack.

A decision was made to send federal employees home. The word was quickly spread that our employees should evacuate the Main State Building. Along with other senior State Department officials, I moved with them to an alternate command site.

Recognizing that there was absolute gridlock in Washington that day, we told the employees not to attempt to retrieve their cars from the basement parking garage. Some simply never would have made it. They were told to find other ways to get home. We were able to manage risk on the run.

It wasn't until days later with the return of some sense of normality that I began to assess what we did right and wrong in response to this moment of uncertainty and how we could have done it better.

One of the many lessons I learned was that in the haste of evacuating the building, we hadn't thought of everything. There had not been an emergency evacuation plan. That was not helpful to the need to care for and help employees with disabilities or handicaps. With the elevator in lockdown, people in wheelchairs or on crutches needed help getting down steps and out of the building. There was no accountability, and some were temporarily left behind at their own risk until the final building sweep was conducted and they were gotten out.

Some things are so simple that they are forgotten. An emergency evacuation plan had slipped the leash of concerns or considerations. Not to have one was unforgivable. The risks that day were everywhere in every way. Our lack of preparedness contributed to the problem.

It didn't take long to fix the problem. I tasked every office to create and display an evacuation diagram and to have a plan that accommodated all the people in the office as they exited the building. We rehearsed the plan quarterly, and the members of each office went to a designated muster point where a head count took place. One less risk to worry about.

Any organization can have and should have a risk management plan. It should be tailored for potential risks in areas of concern to the things that could go wrong when one least expects it. The plan should determine how potential problems should be managed, how they could be mitigated, and how they should be handled if they occur. Risk management is a proactive technique to minimize the effect of threat realization to an organization. It is common practice in business today to do a SWOT analysis, a means of evaluating your *s*trengths, *w*eaknesses, *o*pportunities, and *t*hreats.

Any such analysis needs to be open and honest. An American journalist and founder of the *New Yorker* magazine, Harold Wallace Ross, put risk management in context. He once wrote, "Think as you work, for in the final analysis, your worth to your company comes not only in solving problems, but also anticipating them."

28

Prepare Now for Crisis

Most of us have either heard of or used the expression Murphy's Law: "If something can go wrong, it will." Actually, there was a Murphy, Major Edward A. Murphy, Jr., an American aerospace engineer who worked on safety-critical systems for the air force in the 1940s and 1950s. It is for him that the phrase was coined. When some high-speed rail tests went wrong at Wright-Patterson Field in Ohio, Murphy said, "If there is more than one way to do a job and one of those ways will result in disaster, then someone will do it that way."

Murphy was associated with crisis and found that it's not if but when a crisis will occur. If you accept that to be true, anyone at any time can expect the unexpected. Unwanted circumstances can change your life forever.

Two-thirds of crises should never even make it to the level of crisis. Most are smoldering and should be detected, and if they are, they ought to be dealt with responsibly.

Interestingly and ironically, in August 2001 the Federal Emergency Management Agency (FEMA) conducted an emergency training session to discuss and determine the three most likely catastrophes to strike the United States in the coming years. First on the list was a terrorist attack in New York City. Second was a high-intensity hurricane hitting New Orleans. Third was a major earthquake in the San Andreas Fault.

All three were deemed potential crises. The first shocked the nation and destroyed our sense of invulnerability on September 11, 2001. The second tore a city apart in late August and early September 2005. The third has frightened millions with tremors over time.

FEMA anticipated well these potential crises. Unfortunately, people of responsibility did nothing to prevent or prepare for their happening.

Organizationally, one way to determine the health of an organization's brand is to conduct a crisis audit. That can involve examining business protocols, management actions, or the attitudes of stakeholders. All brands are vulnerable and are defined as much by what others say about them as by what they say about themselves.

The twenty-first century is an era of perception relevance. Organizations can help their cause by having discipline, transparency, and accountability in all they do.

When I was assigned to the United States Military Academy at West Point in 1974, anticipating crisis was the furthest thing from my mind. An institution that had thrived since its founding in 1802, West Point had a pattern of predictability. However, its institutional foundation was shaken in 1975 when President Gerald R. Ford signed into law the admission of women to the three service academies. It became a vexing crisis for them all.

As the media relations officer for the military academy at the time, I experienced an onslaught of media attention. The first class of women entered in July of 1976. Months later, 220 cadets were alleged to have cheated on an electrical engineering exam; 152 were ultimately expelled, but not before enormous institutional scrutiny. It was the largest honor scandal in the history of West Point.

The superintendent of the military academy at the time was the late Lieutenant General Sidney B. Berry, an extraordinarily gifted officer some felt was destined to be the army chief of staff one day. He never rose that far, it could be argued, because of the crises that consumed his tenure as superintendent.

Crisis was in our lives each day as we worked through the tumultuous period of these two challenges. I spent many an hour in General Berry's company working through these two episodes we had never predicted or had crisis plans for. I felt crisis-tested like never before.

That was the case until my phone rang at 6:45 the morning of December 12, 1985. Then the media relations division chief for the U.S. Army, I received a call from the Army Command Center in the Pentagon. I was told that a charter airplane had just crashed upon takeoff from Gander, Newfoundland. Seeking more information, I instinctively turned on the television in my office, and there appeared a Canadian Broadcasting Corporation reporter in a yellow slicker describing the tragedy that lay behind him.

As it turned out, aboard that airplane were 248 soldiers from the 101st Airborne Division and eight crew members from the carrier Arrow Airline. The soldiers were returning to Fort Campbell, Kentucky, from a six-month United Nations peacekeeping assignment in the Sinai. All aboard perished.

This was the largest military air disaster in the nation's history. For me it was a crisis of epic proportions. I learned the hard way about the common elements of a crisis. It occurs with suddenness, it causes time compression, it demands a quick response, it interferes with normal organizational performance, and it creates uncertainty and stress.

For those of us involved, the response was immediate. I installed an 800 number and a bank of telephones in my Pentagon office. I augmented my staff to help answer the flood of calls. A crisis response team was dispatched to Gander by 2 p.m. that day. An investigation into the cause of the crash was launched. Remains were recovered. The next of kin of all who perished were notified.

It was a crisis that went on 24/7 for weeks. As the chief spokesman for the army, I handled hundreds upon hundreds of media inquiries for months. I also had to deal with the mood of the public, which changed from sympathy, to blame, to anger. How could we have used a charter airplane as opposed to one from the U.S. Air Force to ferry our troops home? The answer that the fleet of air force cargo planes was not large enough at the time seemed inadequate. I thought the crisis would never end, and I deeply regretted that the army didn't have a crisis plan for such disasters.

Just as risk management is the proactive approach to unforeseen calamities, crisis management is the reactive response to things that have gone wrong. What kinds of things? Everything from a natural disaster to a technological one and from malevolence to misconduct.

Murphy had it right when he described a major occurrence with a potentially negative outcome. These unwanted events can affect any organization as well as its publics, services, products, or good name.

Because they typically occur with suddenness, such as the events of 9/11, or result in uncertainty, as happened with the nuclear disaster in Chernobyl, Ukraine, in 1986, one needs to have a crisis plan in place beforehand.

Far too many managers and leaders are in denial—it can't happen to us. Not on my watch. Actually, it not only can but probably will happen. Crisis is everywhere and affects organizations in every way.

Smart managers recognize that an organization recovers best when it is prepared for a crisis. You need to help your boss with that form of recognition. You can also persuade the boss to have an ideology that is built on ironclad ethical and professional behavior. Senior managers must have both a plan and procedures in place to execute that plan well.

French general, statesman, and president Charles de Gaulle had it right when he said, "Faced with crisis, the man of character falls back on himself. He imposes his own stamp of action, takes responsibility for it, makes it his own."

29

Be a Strategic Asset

The boss doesn't always know that he or she needs you. He or she may never even ask or think about asking for your help. That doesn't mean you shouldn't provide it as necessary.

If your boss has monumental decisions to make, he or she shouldn't stand alone in that regard. The boss need not do it by herself or himself. Think of yourself as a strategic asset waiting to happen.

If you're waiting to be asked, you're not thinking beyond the moment for the boss, who could probably use your counsel more than he or she thinks. To provide effective counsel you need to be thinking and planning beyond the moment for the things that lie ahead, anticipated or not.

A good way to start is by making an honest appraisal of the business landscape today and what it's likely to look like in the years to come. Understanding what corporate interests are at stake in regard to the decisions you make is key. Knowing your business purposes and the proposed actions for achieving them is also important. Determining the costs, the resources available, and the desired outcomes of those actions is fundamental.

Gubernare is a Latin word meaning "to steer or to control." The term *governance* is the English derivative. You need to be helping the boss steer or govern what he or she should do, how to do it, and why it should be done.

You may have to work yourself into that strategic position. Sound, reasonable advice is the place to start. It may even take a crisis to get the ball rolling.

When Colin Powell became the chairman of Joint Chiefs of Staff in October 1989, I was loaded for bear. He had a sterling reputation as a general, and I set out to burnish that reputation. Regrettably for me, he wasn't quite ready for the public exposure I was offering him.

As I sifted through piles of invitations he received to do one thing or another, I brought the best to the top of the heap. Then I advanced specific recommendations that he accept the very best. He wasn't interested. He needed time to get his sea legs as chairman.

Rejection after rejection over the first three months began to wear on me. I found myself asking what I could do to alter his response. The answer came in mid-December.

He summoned me to his office on December 18, 1989, and said to me, "I need your help. I'm telling you something only a handful of people here in Washington, D.C., know. We're going to invade Panama in two days to take down General Manuel Noriega and the Panama Defense Force." He went on to say, "Obviously this is top secret, but begin planning for the public explanation I will have to make to our stakeholders."

Back in my office I began the strategic thinking and planning I thought necessary. A press conference was going to be essential. Without knowing the absolute outcome of the operation, I prepared for several contingencies. He would probably do this in tandem with the secretary of defense, Dick Cheney. This would be a major moment for both of them. When the United States goes to war, it is big news.

Over the next two days I prepared a variety of things: an opening statement, probable questions from reporters, and proposed answers. Not knowing precisely the details of how the operation would unfold, I chose to be far-ranging on issues I expected to be raised.

He asked me to be back in the building by 11 p.m. on the nineteenth. I went home at the normal time, caught a two-hour nap, and returned to the Pentagon at 10:30 p.m. My best-laid secretive return came as a surprise to one of my assistants, who was working especially late to wrap things up before heading to Alabama for Christmas. I'm not sure who was more surprised, she or I.

Shortly after 11 p.m., I strolled down to the chairman's empty outer office and knocked on his door. Silence. Did I have the wrong day? Quietly I opened the door and peeked in. The boss was stirring from his cat nap. See you in fifteen, he said.

Back I came at 11:20. We headed for the National Military Command Center in a highly secure and classified part of the Pentagon, where we joined the secretary of defense. Plenty of activity in motion: maps, timelines, radios ablaze, many operations and intelligence experts standing at the ready. The chairman took a seat next to Secretary Cheney at a designated command table. They were given the latest ops/intel brief by Lieutenant General Tom Kelly, the senior operations officer, and Rear Admiral Mike McConnell, the senior intelligence officer for the Joint Staff.

On the ground in Panama, there was a sense among the Panama Defense Force (PDF) that something was up. Tactical surprise is essential in combat. Since the PDF was stirring, there was a decision to move the scheduled 1 a.m. H-hour up by 15 minutes. At 0045 hours, Operation Just Cause commenced. A total of 25,000 American troops stationed in Panama, troops from various stateside locations, Delta Force, SEALs, Rangers, you name it, converged on key targets on both the Atlantic and Pacific sides of the Isthmus of Panama.

Night fighting is the most effective form of combat for American troops. The only thing missing when dawn broke was Noriega. He had made a hasty escape to avoid U.S. custody. Evidence of an imperfect world.

By and large, the early stages of Just Cause were successful but required explanation to our stakeholders. That included the public, Congress, American citizens living in Panama, our neighbors in that region, and the world community at large.

Time to go to work. The chairman and I went off into a corner to discuss the likely questions he would be asked in the press conference, how far he could go with his answers while maintaining operational security, and how to explain the AWOL Noriega.

Meanwhile, the secretary spoke to President Bush, who then went on television at 7:40 a.m., still on the twentieth, to explain why we had invaded Panama. Ample evidence of misdeeds by the PDF and missteps by their leader were presented as the rationale.

Cheney and Powell had a brief discussion to ensure they were in sync. At 8:30 a.m. they went together to the Pentagon briefing room to explain details of the operation and next steps. With briefing charts and maps in hand they handled every question adroitly.

For me it was an important event, for it helped solidify the relationship with my boss. He had done the heavy lifting with the prep and brief. Mine was a support role, but it had purpose and lent value to the press briefing.

There doesn't have to be a crisis for the boss to turn to you for well-grounded, well-conceived advice. However, in my case, it helped reinforce the contribution I could make to prepare him for delivering strategic and tactical decisions to the publics to which we were responsible. That request for assistance by the boss doesn't just happen, and when it does happen, it doesn't guarantee there will be routine reliance on you.

Strategic management needs to take place on a regular basis. Strategic thinking and strategic planning need to be part of your professional portfolio. As Dwight Eisenhower once said, "Plans are nothing; planning is everything." The value of the planning you do for what lies ahead is an asset your boss will come to rely on, to expect, and to count on as part of separating your organization from the competition. That's a form of relevance you can and should claim in the life of your boss.

30

Don't Hesitate to Tell the Boss
He or She Is Wrong

There's nothing worse than not wanting to roll out of bed in the morning and head for work. Many people feel that way. Some let their friends know when they get there that they'd rather be anyplace else, doing anything else, for anyone else.

Instead of feeling like it's a wonderful world, they feel downright blue about their place in life. Someone once said, "The biggest troublemaker you'll probably have to deal with watches you from the mirror every morning." That may be true, and if it is, you're the only one who can fix it. New town, new company, new job, new boss? Any and all of those alternatives are possible. But maybe what you really need is a new start and a new attitude.

However, when it's less about you than it is about your boss, that presents a different and more difficult problem. If the boss is here to stay, invest in determining what is wrong and how to fix it. That might require an attitude adjustment in terms of accepting the boss—right or wrong, good or bad—as the person who calls the shots.

Over the course of my professional life, I couldn't wait to get to work, do my job, and do it well. Success at it was my reward, and I have found that success begets success. It can also be shared with others who work for you so that their mood and motivation match yours.

Along the way I hit a bump in the road. My old boss, whom I admired and respected, retired. My new boss, who was admired for what he had previously achieved professionally in his life, was totally out of his element. No experience in this newly assigned field yet put there because of his overall reputation up to that point.

It didn't take long for a collision to occur on this particular road of life we were on together. He was very self-assured and outspoken in his views. It was in the third week or so of the morning staff meetings he chaired, and a dozen or so of his senior assistants attended. We were gathered in his Pentagon office when the confrontation occurred.

As the chief of media relations for the army, I apprised him of a press report critical of the army on a particular issue. "That's the problem," he barked. "The press reports things as they want to see them, not as they actually are." Careful, I thought to myself; hold your tongue. The relationship with my new boss was young. No need to damage it at such an early stage or at all.

He went on to say, "If it hadn't been for a critical press, we would have won the war in Vietnam." As a Vietnam veteran aviator, he saw it from his point of view. As a Vietnam veteran infantryman, I saw it differently. We didn't lose the war; we simply didn't win it, not because of our tactical inadequacies or failures in the field but because of our strategic incompetence at the national level. He was wrong with the glittering generalities he put forward in a heated and pointed way. For a good part of that meeting and on subsequent occasions it was evident that he had a beef with the press.

Clearly he saw me as part of the problem. Since to his way of thinking I dealt each day with those dastardly reporters, I must be on the side of the enemy. At least I sensed he believed that.

There were numerous clashes when he and I simply did not agree. He had a slight advantage—he was a general, I was a colonel. I paid him his due respect, but I never hesitated to tell him when I thought he was wrong, always giving him the reasons for my point of view.

One might argue that when you are at odds with the boss, silence is sometimes the tactically best answer, and that may be so if you choose harmony over honesty. You are never going to move the needle, however, if you don't express your opinion on things you feel strongly about or, better yet, you know to be true.

I parted company with my general and boss who hated the press a year or so later and went to a much better job working for a man far more understanding of the role of the press in a democratic society. Ironically, years later the general with whom I never saw eye to eye tracked me down telephonically. He had retired and had been asked to look for a candidate to work as public relations counsel for former President Ronald Reagan at his official office in California.

I thanked him for his interest in considering me but declined, telling him I had a job I enjoyed immensely. It did my heart good, however, to realize that despite our disagreements in days past, he felt confident enough in my skill set to offer it up to the president. Perhaps, just perhaps, my honesty was one of the qualities that passed his litmus test.

Not that any two circumstances or relationships with bosses are the same. But one thing is a constant: the openness and honesty you need to have with your boss when that person is not correct or is not using proper judgment.

If you tactfully explain to that person what is not right or needs to be done differently, he or she may well respect you and your opinion more than would be the case if you never offered it. No one likes to be told they are wrong, but if they're smart, they'll prefer that to making a mistake.

31

If at First Your Opinion
Doesn't Succeed, Try, Try Again

How many times have you heard or used the expression "If at first you don't succeed, try, try again"? It might have been when you were hovering over a homework assignment with a parent, hearing a teacher offer encouragement in the classroom, or listening to a coach on the athletic field.

Actually, there is a second part to that popular quote, courtesy of author-comedian W. C. Fields, who completed the thought by saying, "Then quit. There's no point in being a darn fool about it." He might have been joking, but he certainly knew what he was talking about. Or did he?

For those who have access to the boss and his or her thinking, a cardinal rule is to be honest with the boss. Anything less is unhelpful and of little value. Building a relationship of trust and confidence is important in that regard. Offering alternatives to the boss's thoughts or decisions is essential. Identifying a problem is invaluable; providing a solution is essential.

Bosses may not like or appreciate it when they are offered a critique or rebuttal, but if they value the outcome of their decision making, they should listen and learn so that they benefit the most. For your part, the prospect of getting yelled at or kicked out of the office should live in the corner of your mind at moments like this but should not deter you from making your voice heard.

Back in the fall of 1991 such a moment, actually moments, occurred for me. My office phone rang one September morning, and I answered it to hear the voice and plea of the late CBS *60 Minutes* reporter Ed Bradley. "I'd like to interview your boss," he said. "Why so?" I asked. "Because he's an American hero and the public deserves to know him better, especially after the successful Gulf War he helped orchestrate," responded Bradley.

We discussed briefly the merits of his request, and I told Bradley, a highly respected broadcast journalist, that I'd get back to him after discussing it with the boss, Joint Chiefs chairman Colin Powell. As was the protocol, I prepared a memo with the details and offered a recommendation that he agree to the interview.

To my surprise, he put his initials on the "Decline" line at the bottom of the memo. For purposes of elaboration I went with memo in hand to his office to ask for his reason and his reconsideration. "I just don't want to do it," said Powell. Too many interviews, too little time for other requirements of the office.

Retreating to my office a bit wounded, though not fatally, I pondered the issue. This could be an opportunity to praise the 541,000 men and women who had achieved victory in the 43 days of combat during Operation Desert Storm earlier that year.

A few days elapsed, and I summoned the courage to request an audience to tell the boss I thought he was wrong about his twice-chosen declination. In the quiet of his office, just he and I, my appeal emphasized his chance to tell the American people how great the troops had been. Standing at the corner of his desk, I offered my rationale that it was about them, not him. His look was stern. He slammed his fist on the desktop and said sharply, "Goddammit, Smullen, I do everything you ask me to do."

This was my opening, and I knew my last chance, maybe forever if he fired me for persistence. "Yes, sir, and I'll never ask you to do anything that I don't think is right," was my retort. Silence, pause, then, "Okay, I'll do it," he said with more than a bit of exasperation in his voice.

Before he could change his mind I hastily departed, rushed to my office, called Bradley, and told him we were on. "Hooray" was his reaction. We talked details of the when and where. An hour later the chairman buzzed me on the intercom. "Have you spoken to Bradley yet?" he asked. "Yes, sir," I answered. "Damn!" he replied before hanging up with a bang.

Knowing my credibility was on the line, I called Bradley's producer, Marley Klaus, and invited her to visit me in the Pentagon for her research. It was my attempt to move the interview in a direction that wouldn't get me fired and would make the boss—but more important the troops—look good. She agreed and spent a day with me in the Pentagon asking good questions.

The interview actually took place in Vancouver, Washington, on November 8, 1991, after General Powell gave the annual Marshall Lecture sponsored by the George C. Marshall Foundation.

We flew to Vancouver the day of the event. The good news was that General Powell was an admirer of General Marshall and so looked forward to the talk. The bad news was that in flight on a dedicated air force jet taking us to our destination, the chairman motioned for me to come forward to his cabin. "Smullen," he said, "I don't know how I let you talk me into this. I have a cold, I don't feel good, and I'm not looking forward to the interview with Bradley." Knowing that at 30,000 feet there was no place to hide from his disapproval, I stood my ground and assured him there was considerable benefit to the upcoming venture.

After the lecture and a talk he gave to some students at a local school, both of which Bradley's crew filmed, the general retired to the quaint home on the campus of Fort Vancouver National Site, formerly Vancouver U.S. Army Barracks, where Marshall was stationed and lived from 1936 to 1938.

Bradley sat waiting in the living room of this historic home Marshall had occupied as the installation commander back then.

He greeted Powell, who took a seat opposite him. I straightened the general's tie and wished I could straighten his strained and wary look, one that cried out, "Let the pain be over."

Relief was on the way as Bradley asked his first question about challenges to black men and women growing up in the Hunts Point section of the Bronx in the days of Powell's youth. The general's strained expression softened; he smiled and even chuckled before answering that that was where he got his start in life. An artful icebreaker by a crafty broadcast journalist; that research offer to Bradley's producer had paid off.

The piece aired on January 12, 1992. It was heavily promoted during the professional football game televised on CBS before *60 Minutes* that Sunday. No pressure there! As air time grew near, I got more nervous. If this went south, I'd probably go with it.

The segment was the first to air that night on *60 Minutes*. It was long, it was good, it came as a relief. It had no sooner ended than my phone rang. It was the chairman. "Did you see it?" he asked. "Yes, sir." "What did you think?" "I liked it," was all I could get out before he said, "So did I; thanks for asking me to do it."

Whew! I'd live to fight another day. There's no point in being a damn fool about it, Mr. Fields, but there is a point in sticking up for what you feel is right, in speaking out with your best advice.

To achieve something you never had, you may have to do something you've never done or have never wanted to do. That may mean telling the boss he or she's wrong; it may mean walking softly but speaking smartly about what is best for the organization, which is the most important thing of all.

32

Expect the Unexpected

Age and experience serve as sources for better anticipating what lies ahead. As twice-over British Prime Minister Benjamin Disraeli said in the nineteenth century, "The expected always happens." For the most part that's true; it's the unexpected that poses a problem.

That doesn't mean you have to check under every rock or peer around every corner all the time to see what's there. But you do need to take a regular sensing of what is occurring in your work world that you didn't anticipate. Why? Because it's smart. Moreover, it allows your reflexes to catch what's coming your way.

If you have responsibilities in the office that go beyond just you, this extra vision comes in handy for others. Who might that be? Your subordinates, your peers, and most of all your boss. He or she has a hefty magnitude of responsibility already. In most cases, the boss has more to do than anyone else. The boss could use your help, oh, by the way. You can tell the boss you'll be on the lookout for asteroids or earthquakes. Or you can just do it because it's the right thing to do.

Large or small, threatening or not, the unexpected is going to be part of your professional life. You hold the cards and can determine the stakes.

Sometimes this comes naturally to people with responsibility; sometimes they have to work at it. Either way it's part of your job description, written or assumed.

Over the course of my career, I had ample opportunity to provide those kinds of responses for the people I served. I didn't always see things coming, but I improved at doing so as I learned to anticipate better the world around me and recognized the value of doing so. This came in handy in 1995 as Colin Powell and I finished the five-week "mother of all book tours" to promote his memoirs, *My American Journey*, and returned to our offices in Alexandria, Virginia, seeking a return to normalcy.

Not so fast! No rest for the weary. There had been ample outreach and encouragement by the thousands who paraded before him on the book tour. They wanted a signed book, but they were also asking that he run for president. Unexpected and unasked for admiration for a man they apparently felt they could trust.

He had an unexpected decision to make. Should he yield to this onslaught of political speculation and encouragement to declare his candidacy and run for president?

It sounds like an admirable thing to do. It plays to your ego. It conjures up all sorts of imperial fantasies of what life in the White House would be like. It also scares the hell out of you.

Over time, I have been asked several thousand times, "Why didn't he make a run for it?" I have thought the answer through as many times or more. To start with, this was totally unanticipated. He didn't ask to be president, he didn't position himself to be a candidate; it just happened. The American people fell in love with Colin Powell going back to his days as chairman of the Joint Chiefs, and that was very flattering. However, as the general always did when making an important decision, he considered all the factors. Not the least of these were the uncertainties and the unknowns. There were many.

Money. Since it would take tens of millions of dollars to run a primary campaign and hundreds of millions to run an entire presidential campaign, where would that kind of money come from?

He hadn't even declared a party affiliation. It's a tougher financial climb for an independent. Between the two of us, we surely did not have the financial means to conduct a political campaign.

Timing. It was November 1995. For a general election that would take place in November 1996, he would have to declare his intent to run by December 1995, choose a party, and register for the primaries that would begin taking place in February 1996. That would have been a lot of work to accomplish in the short time available.

Staffing. When you have a staff of two, myself and one other, it seems a little light on people power. You need dozens and dozens of experts. We didn't have that, and we had little time to raise a qualified staff. Not just people who wanted to help, not just well-meaning volunteers, but people who knew what they were doing when it came to political campaigns.

Policies. We had not one policy, foreign or domestic. We knew a lot about a lot of things, but for the most part that didn't include well-developed positions on matters of importance to the people. I knew we couldn't just make it up as we went along.

Space. With a small suite of offices, four in number, we were ill prepared to house the people who would be necessary to run a successful campaign. A campaign headquarters needs to be large and bustling, a place where hundreds of people can set up shop if necessary.

Family. When you run for president, it's about more than just you. It's about your spouse, children, even grandchildren. It's about friend and foe alike. If you are elected president, it's about those people in your life now but also about those who will be affected for the rest of their lives: where they live, where they go, what they do, who goes with them to protect them. You are a president until you die. Those important people in your life are affected that long or longer and deserve a vote too.

Aspiration. Soldiers don't want to grow up to be cowboys or even presidents. It's simply not in their DNA. We were just two old soldiers trying to sell a book. When you don't have a desire to be someone or something in life, you can't fake it. Call it a fire in the belly, call it a need, call it what you will. If your heart's not in it, it's a tough sell to oneself.

I had not expected the unexpected, the unwanted. But overwhelming political attention on Powell during the book tour left no doubt in my mind that the public insistence on his running would not go away. We would have to answer the call and very soon.

When the tour was over, I called a handful of people who had called me earlier that year saying they could find money if he made a run for it. They told me they stood ready to help. I circled back to dozens of friends who said they would volunteer to help if I ever needed them. All reassured me that they were ready. I found an entire empty floor in our office building. It was available and could be built out to house a staff.

Not perfect, but so far, so good. Timing was out of my hands, but the clock was still ticking. I could not change the dates of the primaries. Policy positions were endless: everything from the needs of wheat farmers in the Midwest to how to handle despots around the world. Data not easily assembled in the time available. As far as family and friends, no support parades had formed there.

The most important thing of all was his degree of desire to become president. I couldn't be sure of this from one day to the next. Some days, I'd sense that yes, he was going for it; other days, no way, no how. Still the planning went on, down to and including a place where he could make his announcement one way or the other. The general manager of a hotel three blocks from our office was sworn to secrecy, but he agreed to be ready for a press conference on one day's notice.

Anxious days. Sleepless nights. An unannounced weight loss program. Both of us sensed the gravity of the moment and the fact that the decision could be life-changing. Not once did he ask my opinion. Sometimes that's how friends are.

Time was slipping by, and at the end of day on Friday, November 3, I went into his office and closed the door. Darkness had fallen. The room seemed eerily quiet. I said, "General, you have not asked for my opinion, but I owe you these thoughts. If you choose to go, I'm with you all the way." But I gave him several considerations I thought he needed to ponder strongly before making his decision.

They included family, friends, finances, policies and positions on issues, and the obvious distraction from efforts to promote his book. I added, "I'm not convinced you should be headed in the direction of running." He nodded and said he'd take it aboard.

The following Monday night he called me at home with his decision. He had decided against making a run. He felt comfortable with his choice not to seek the presidency. I urged him to make that conclusion public soon but to give me two days to make the final arrangements. On Tuesday, I issued a widespread telephonic press advisory indicating that the general intended to hold a press conference the following day at midafternoon in the ballroom of the hotel I had chosen earlier for the venue.

On November 8, 1995, he stood before a bank of reporters. With his wife, Alma, at his side on a stage that had been erected, he told the group that after serious consideration he had decided against running. He spoke about the impact that entry into political life would have on him and his family. He cited the sacrifices and difficulties required. He said, "The welfare of my family had to be the uppermost in my mind. Ultimately, however, I had to look deep into my soul, standing aside from the expectations and enthusiasms of others." He concluded by saying, "I do not yet have a passion for political life, because such a life requires a calling that I do not yet hear." At the end, however, he declared himself a Republican. It answered a lingering question many had asked.

He and I both slept better that night. We even started eating properly again. Yes, he had disappointed many millions of Americans. He regretted having done that. It had taken courage to not run, but it came with the conviction that first and foremost this needed to be about what was right for him.

For me the lessons were many. In life there is no clear road map for what lies ahead, no GPS system to guide us to a precise destination. Anticipation is very helpful. Had I not anticipated and had he decided to seek public office, the road ahead for both of us could have been highly uncertain and rocky.

As with an oncoming storm, you consider all the kinds of impacts this natural disaster can have on you. High winds, torrential rains, potential flooding, damage to property, loss of power and services, safety for self and others as well is most critical. Apply the same logic to all those things coming your way at high speed in the work world that could be destabilizing.

Preparing for that uncertainty is the key. Intuition is reliable. Considering all that could happen whether programmed or not. Allowing yourself to be all-inclusive with considerations of the things that can happen near term and long term in life. The kinds of things you can do for yourself and for your boss.

It doesn't mean you have to be a fretter or a worrywart. It doesn't mean you should overwhelm your boss with high-anxiety concerns. It does mean that you should be a thinker with the capacity to deal with things headed your way. Yes, we had expected that he'd sign a lot of books on the tour—60,000 to be exact. However, we had not expected the political frenzy that had encompassed us. It was important to translate those things into good advice for the boss, who hadn't had time to expect the unexpected.

33

Inspire the Right Work Ethic

Too often we make things more difficult than they need to be or should be. That tends to be too frequently true of sound ethics in the workplace.

I'm not sure why, because it's a pretty simple issue. There is nothing difficult about differentiating between right and wrong. Yet the business page of any major newspaper is full of examples of people of responsibility in the business world violating the law by one or another unethical or unlawful practice.

Striving to do the right thing in a highly complex and competitive world leads to temptations some find irresistible. Instead of creating and maintaining a healthy corporate culture with an established code of conduct, some leaders and managers are driven in the opposite direction by greed, dishonesty, or misconduct. It's a pity if the next promotion or bottom-line profits steer your actions in the wrong direction.

Having a reliable work ethic is about having a set of values and accompanying virtues that guide an organization's decisions and its respect for those inside and outside the company, employees and customers alike. William Shakespeare said it well: "Love all, trust a few, do wrong to none."

Leaders set the standard, senior managers enforce the standard, subordinates follow the standard. Trust in all three categories to do the right thing can and should be natural and expected.

The Institute for Global Ethics puts ethical values in more precise terms with respect to business dealings, transactions, relationships, and situations. It emphasizes five areas or indexes of importance: to be honest and truthful, responsible and accountable, fair and equitable, respectful and mindful, and compassionate and caring.

Pretty good yardsticks that came in handy in June 1998 to measure the ethical veracity of an explosive report on *NewsStand*, a new prime-time magazine-format program launched on Sunday, June 7, by CNN. One segment, titled "Valley of Death," featured an eight-month investigation by CNN and *TIME* magazine into the alleged use of lethal nerve gas during the Vietnam War.

Veteran CNN correspondent Peter Arnett described how a secret elite unit of U.S. Special Forces had carried out Operation Tailwind, a 1970 mission to kill American soldiers who had defected to the enemy. Arnett told how commandos approached a Laotian village where the American defectors had been spotted by reconnaissance units. "During the evening," Arnett reported, "American planes gassed the camp with deadly sarin nerve gas."

Having had two tours in Vietnam and having seen and been on military operations as both an advisor and part of an American unit, I had never witnessed nor could I imagine anything so despicable. Not only would it have been illegal and in violation of the Geneva Conventions, to have killed fellow Americans would have been unthinkable.

My phone lit up two days later when the caller, retired air force Major General Perry Smith, asked if I had seen the program. A CNN military analyst for several years, he expressed outrage over not having been consulted before what he viewed as not just an inaccurate but an untrue account. A respected analyst, Smith knew about such things as a decorated fighter pilot who had flown 180 missions and had 370 combat hours in Vietnam. He knew full well that pilots everywhere during the war knew the type ordnance they were carrying and did or didn't drop. Furthermore, he knew that munitions records validated the types of missions pilots were flying over Vietnam, Laos, or Cambodia during the Vietnam War.

Smith, whom I had known for years and for whom I had great respect, asked if I'd share his concerns with my boss, General Colin Powell, whom he knew well. Further, he said that if Powell agreed with him, he should call Tom Johnson, CNN News Group chairman, president, and CEO. Powell and Johnson had been White House Fellows together in an earlier time.

When General Powell returned days later from a trip, I shared the CNN report and subsequent news stories that were especially critical of and damaging to the image of the U.S. military. The general and I doubted the CNN claims that deadly nerve gas had been used, killing soldiers and innocent women and children. This would have meant that war crimes had been committed by U.S. forces during Tailwind, as it was called.

Powell unhesitatingly called Johnson and warned him that the validity of the report was highly suspect and that if it was not retracted, it probably would cast aspersions on CNN. Johnson agreed to check into the story. They talked again two days later. Johnson expressed confidence in the report, having discussed it with Arnett and the primary producer of the segment, April Oliver.

Meanwhile, the defense secretary, William Cohen, ordered an investigation by the department into the allegations. The investigators found no evidence that nerve gas was ever used anywhere in the theater during the Vietnam War. Johnson and CNN came under blistering attack from watchdog groups and citizens alike.

Citing his inexplicable lack of involvement in the development of the piece, the serious damage to the U.S. military and U.S. foreign policy because of the report, and the threat to the credibility of CNN for developing a hypothesis it didn't attempt to disaffirm, Perry Smith resigned on June 14. That took courage and conviction.

Truth has a way of rising to the surface when a question of ethics is raised. Clearly it was with CNN and with *TIME* as well, which published a "Did the U.S. Drop Nerve Gas?" article on June 15. It was a breathless but baseless headline that drew fire.

Tom Johnson meanwhile had gone back to look more deeply into the allegations. His internal investigation had concluded that the Tailwind report could not be supported and that there was insufficient evidence that sarin or any other deadly gas had been used. On July 2 he issued a 54-page CNN retraction and a statement that said, "Nothing is more important to a news organization than its reputation for accuracy, fairness and responsibility."

The fallout within CNN was significant. Two key CNN producers of the report, April Oliver and Jack Smith, were fired outright. Senior producer Pam Hill resigned. Reporter Peter Arnett was reprimanded and soon left for HDNet and then NBC. Oliver and Smith filed lawsuits against their former employer. Their cases were settled out of court.

Justice had been served by the discipline meted out by CNN. However, the institutional damage to the U.S. military had marred its reputation. Had higher ethical standards existed at CNN/*TIME*, had better oversight occurred, had there been surer accountability, this damaging report might have never aired.

For the CNN/*TIME* family, it was a lesson in organizational humiliation. For me, it was a lesson in the need for the existence of organizational values. Having a code of ethical behavior is crucial to every professional and every organization. Such a code stands on traditional virtues that form a foundation built on trust, honesty, and a commitment to do the right thing. Doing so can avoid conflicts of interest that cause the wrong thing to happen.

As a professional, regardless of rank or position, you must be accountable for all you do or fail to do to uphold the reputation and credibility of the organization. That may come naturally to those who were raised to uphold the highest of ethical and moral standards. Others may have to learn it.

Increasingly common in organizations in the United States are established ethics programs. Ideally, they are conducted annually and are for all employees regardless of rank or time on the job. They are harmless, and they are timeless. Broad in content, they should be updated to remain current.

The benefits are far-ranging. Recruits are inspired by it. Current employees are satisfied by it. Company reputations are improved by it. It's a painless investment that retains people and reminds them of company expectations.

Employees who feel valued by the organization as a result of ethics training are less likely to break the rules or the law. They are also more likely to report the misconduct of others. To accept less is to accept a low standard.

As a conscience for your organization, and each of us is, you have a responsibility to look at how the place runs, at those who run it, and at what the organization stands for and behind. That starts with the boss, but it includes the rank and file as well. Every day you work and everything you do during the day offers moments of truth as to what is ethically correct. Ethical dilemmas are sometimes unavoidable; compromise of the highest ethical standards possible is always unacceptable.

You can stand out at work as one who has a values-based work ethic: one with purpose and power, one that gives you the confidence and courage to make good choices. You can inspire others above, below, and around you by serving as a shining example of someone who makes the right choices in life. You can help create the right ethical climate in your organization; you'll be glad you did.

34

Reflect a Front Office
That Is Cheerful

Most organizations have a front office or its equivalent. Typically it is occupied by some of the most important people in the organization: everyone from a receptionist, a secretary, or a personal assistant to a special assistant, a chief of staff, a speechwriter, or anyone the boss wants close by.

These people may have separate offices or cubicles or their own work spaces in one form or another, but collectively they are the face of the organization. From welcoming outsiders as they enter the office to being the phone voice who greets people long distance, they are the beginning of a critical moment in time. Whether it's the one who greets you with a handshake or the one who greets you with a chat, they represent the start of a conversation or even a relationship.

No matter the title or the position, no matter the place or the space, these are undeniable, indelible first impressions. As the expression goes, you never get a second chance to make a first impression.

It's not their charm that matters most; it's their attitude. That could be something as simple as the tone of their voice, the first words they express, a sincere smile, or a firm handshake.

An important part of what you project in person is the way you are dressed. Dressing for success isn't just for interviews or sales meetings. It is an everyday standard that should be set high.

My personal goal was to always have a well-designed, well-fitting suit, a freshly starched shirt, a stylish tie, and shoes that were shined and the right color to match the suit. As I sat down for each and every meeting, my goal was simple—to be the best dressed I could be. Take pride when someone comments favorably on your clothing. When it comes to attire, it's okay to find ways to express yourself so that it reflects well on the office and the boss.

That positive reflection is just as important for the other employees who are bringing something to the front office that was requested or coming forward for a meeting. They may be dropping by because they have something to offer in the way of input or just to say hello.

For internal and external publics alike, the front office is a reflection of the boss. It is actually an indicator of what lies beyond this important nerve center: what goes on inside the C-suite.

It is fairly easy to reflect a good mood or a sense of goodwill when all is going well. It's not nearly as easy when something wrong has happened or a crisis has occurred. It's during times like those that an upbeat, positive attitude should and must be projected. If it is not, the foul mood of the moment spreads far and wide to others.

Having inherited people who were more negative about life than was helpful, I've had to correct "woe is me!" attitudes. I have tried everything from encouragement to counseling in hopes of changing negatives to positives.

I've had to ask a "frontline face" to treat everyone the same—positively. If you can't represent the boss properly and positively, I'll trade you for another. I don't need you. You're no help to me. In fact, you are a liability.

When a dear friend of mine was experiencing personal turmoil, I called to express my concern and offer my support. I was confronted with his personal assistant, who projected a tone of voice that was sad. She knew about the difficulties, but instead of expressing fealty and full support for her boss, she did just the opposite: she sounded depressed and dispirited. If an unaware caller had heard her, he or she would have immediately sensed that something was wrong. This was not helpful to her boss.

"Be it the best of times or the worst of times," to paraphrase Charles Dickens, it is professionalism that carries you to a better place. It's not about faking it. It's not about minimizing it. It's not about ignoring it. It's about being professional, and that means maintaining balance, being composed, and never letting on that you're not maintaining consistency.

If someone, anyone, walks into the life of the organization, whether in person or by phone, you just might be the first person he or she sees or talks to. In keeping with the biblical recommendation to "be of good cheer," be upbeat and sincere. The boss may never know you are reflecting those good traits, but he or she will be forever grateful.

The feedback may come to your boss in the form of a compliment about the staff or even about you personally. Your boss may benefit by establishing a new stakeholder relationship. It may even be about new business. Whatever the benefit, your boss will sense that you had a part in it.

Who knows, you might even be the unexpected beneficiary in the form of a simple compliment, high praise, or even a bonus, raise, or promotion. But don't anticipate feedback from the boss. When you think about it, he or she should expect what you do well to be done each and every day.

In return, your boss will know when his or her frontline staff hasn't represented him or her well. That is a moment worth avoiding.

35

Impress Early and Often

Unless you're a recluse or happen to be socially inept, you spend more of your life, both personally and professionally, interacting with people than doing anything else. It's the social animal in you at work.

The family and friends side of socializing is more natural and carefree than the routine or irregular interaction you have with people at work. Those workplace folks come in an assortment of categories: superiors, subordinates, peers, customers, clients, and a wide variety of stakeholders with whom you typically interface.

For most people, socializing comes with the territory; it's a routine part of a day at the office. Others have to work at it either because they don't consider it important or because they can't be bothered with expending the effort.

The person with whom it matters most is the boss. It's worth putting forth the effort to impress, which by definition is "to affect deeply or strongly in mind." That is particularly relevant when either the boss or you are new. If that is the case, it pays to impress early and often to influence the boss's opinion of you.

It's a natural challenge to be successful when the relationship is fresh. A helpful start is to do your homework to determine not only what the new boss is like but what his or her priorities are. Make them yours as well.

Show the boss you are an absolute professional in each and every way. Part of that is letting the boss know and see that you're committed to achieving the goals and expectations he or she has established.

Be genuine about it but learn how to think and act like the boss. The boss will recognize the results of your efforts as being a vital asset to the company's mission.

Make your boss's job easy. Whether it's an assigned task or one that you do because it needs to be done and can make a measureable difference, do it with enthusiasm and commitment. You need not brag about mission accomplished; the boss will see and appreciate what you've done on his or her own.

Ensure that the boss has to tell you only once what to do or what he or she wants. Take whatever it is off the boss's plate of things to accomplish. Be a load lightener, and it will be appreciated.

At a midpoint in my military career as a major, I needed a particular infantry assignment to remain competitive. Being sent to Fort Carson, Colorado, was a great first step. I fully expected to be assigned as an executive officer (XO) of one of the several infantry battalions in the 4th Infantry Division.

For some reason, a member of Congress froze the U.S. Army's lieutenant colonel promotion list just as I arrived in Colorado Springs. That meant the majors in those executive officer billets in the division remained in their jobs, precluding majors like me from moving into those choice assignments.

Needing a job and after a bit of pleading, I was assigned to the next higher level, an infantry brigade, as a staff officer. The good news was that it was with the best brigade in the division; the bad news was that it was as a personnel officer or adjutant, as it is known. Not my cup of tea.

My new boss, the brigade commander, was a colonel whose reputation was golden. My duties basically involved sitting outside his office doing the administrative chores he directed or needed.

Like anything I did, it was done to the best of my ability, serving every professional need the boss had and every personnel need the brigade had. That required countless trips into the colonel's office each day to discuss requisite actions.

Occasionally, I'd mention to or remind my boss that my ultimate goal was to be one level closer to the troops as a battalion executive officer. His response was always the same. "You're doing a great job where you are, and I need your services here," he'd say. Not exactly what I hoped to hear.

Barely two months had passed when the promotion list was finally approved by Congress and reassignments were possible. One opening was in the 1st Battalion, 12th Infantry Regiment, one of the most highly regarded battalions on post.

Fortunately, I didn't have far to go to speak to the person controlling who went where. My boss was the decider of such fiercely competitive matters.

Hat in hand, I walked into his office the next day and told him, "Sir, it's a privilege working for you, but being with soldiers at the unit level is what I want and, more importantly, need from a professional development standpoint." After what seemed like hours after my passionate plea, he conceded by saying, "Reluctantly I'll let you go, but only because you have earned it with your commitment to this job and to me."

Whew! Free at last to get my boots muddy again and to be down with soldiers at the battalion level, the best job of all.

After an exciting and fulfilling year as a battalion XO, I was reassigned as the chief of plans and operations for the division, a plum but exceptionally demanding job. For 22 months, a division record at the time, I was operationally tested and survived the long hours and demanding days.

Three jobs in three years. All different, all special in their own ways. A lot of luck no doubt, but indicative that someone was always watching and must have been impressed with what they saw.

For each job you have or get, come prepared each day to do the best you know how. It also helps to come early and stay late, within reason; it will set you apart in all probability. In the same vein, pack your lunch. It helps control the intake, and because it takes less time than going out to lunch, it controls the output. Minimum downtime is a good goal.

Take pride in taking the initiative without being asked. Come prepared each day to accomplish more than expected. It will draw the right attention.

Not everything will go perfectly, but try not to complain; it'll always get better. Maintaining a positive attitude will help contribute to that cause. That attitude can be infectious and will move the ball down the field to the delight of the boss.

Positive first impressions count for a lot. A firm handshake, a bright smile. It's good for business. Lasting impressions of the right kind have long-term value. They build and maintain relationships whether with the boss or with the many stakeholders who are of great importance to the boss and to the company. Keep planting those seeds of friendship, for they will bear a harvest of goodwill.

36

Keep Meetings
to 30 Minutes or Less

Have you ever called someone during business hours and been told that that person was in a meeting? That's fine. "A return call will do" is the typical response.

Time goes by; actually a lot of time normally goes by, and the return call finally comes. The person apologetically says, "So sorry; I've been in meetings all day." It happens to the best of us, the meeting part, that is.

As frustrating as that delay is for the original caller, it's a guarantee that the person who was being called, who has been trapped in those meetings, is the real victim. Increasingly, meetings are the norm. Lots of them and for long periods. Statistically, most chief executives spend nearly a third of their workweek in meetings.

One of my favorite bosses was the late Colonel Thomas P. Garigan. He was the public affairs officer at West Point in the mid-1970s. Tom was smart in so many ways. One of them was the frequency and length of the staff meetings he held.

He had a proverb displayed prominently on the table in his office. It said, "No meeting shall last longer than necessary."

Tom lived by this and made his staff live by it too. We were delighted.

As his media relations officer, I had plenty of business to attend to. Much of it was outside the office, escorting reporters or sitting in on interviews. Taking time for a meeting was problematic for me. Fortunately, there weren't many to contend with.

From that point on, Tom Garigan's rule became my rule. Hold meetings infrequently and keep them to a minimum. The frequency part is easy. Have them only when you need them and have something to say or share. As for the length of the meeting, my rule is simple: keep meetings to 30 minutes or less if at all possible.

Why? If it takes more than 30 minutes, there had better be a crisis to deal with. If not, you ought to be able to handle most matters in a half hour or less.

That's easily done if you are the one who has called the meeting. How? Keep the number of attendees down to only those who are essential. This is particularly helpful advice if you are managing a meeting for the boss. Limit the seats at the table to those who deserve or need one.

Unfortunately, you can't always control the behavior of those at the table. Nothing can kill the mood of a meeting more quickly than a dominator, someone who disrupts or monopolizes the conversation. Another killer is a rambler, one who takes the conversation to places that have little or no relevance to the subject.

There are plenty of naysayers in the world, and if one happens to attend your meeting, she or he can prolong the discussion just by projecting negativity. The deadliest attendee of all is one who seeks attention by cracking jokes or trying to sound funny when he or she's not. It ruins the mood of the meeting and the flow of conversation.

Then there are those who fall hostage to their portable electronic devices and spend more time checking their e-mail than contributing to the conversation. They don't consume time as much as waste it. "No device" bans need to be erected to curb these culprits.

With respect to an agenda, create one and distribute it to the attendees at least a day in advance. Prioritize the items to be discussed so that the most important ones get early and full deliberation. Let all the attendees know the timeline and the expectation to be punctual, to be engaged, and to be crisp in making their points.

The punctual part requires everyone to be on time for the prescribed start of the meeting. One way to encourage that is to lock the door as the meeting starts; latecomers are denied access.

This is all easy if you are in charge of the meeting. If you are simply an attendee and want to help with the flow of the meeting, you may have to be creative. Checking your watch every few minutes might not endear you to the organizer of the meeting.

If you are truly pressed for time, let the person who called the meeting know in advance that you have only so much time to devote to the meeting or that you have a pressing conflict. If the meeting minutes are posted later, you will not have lost anything; in fact, you will have gained something—time.

At some organizations people are becoming so anal when it comes to cutting down on time spent in company meetings that everyone has to stand. Sitting and nonwork chitchat are viewed as unacceptable. The object of standing tall is to eliminate long-winded dissertations. Some have found that holding their meetings with people standing, especially meetings held near lunchtime, reduces meeting time by a third.

Why is all this important? Because time is one of the most important resources in your life. It can be a friend or a foe. If you lose time or waste time, you abuse time. This is especially important for the boss, normally the busiest person of all.

Keep time on your side. Keep those meetings to a minimum in terms of frequency and duration. You will be glad you did. The person who will appreciate it most is your boss, who is paying you to be the most productive you can be. He or she may even agree with the unknown author who said, "Ordinary people think merely of spending time. Great people think of using it."

If you are in the middle of an organizational crisis, all bets are off. You may need to meet often and for long periods to strategize and plan a way forward.

During such crisis periods, you actually are apt to lose any sense of time. Hours may seem like minutes, and days may simply dissolve into the seemingly endless time it takes to solve the problem. That may take weeks or months. That may also entail meetings galore. Whatever it takes on crisis occasions is time well spent.

37

Provide the Boss Some Cover

In the military vernacular, *cover* means to lay down a base of firepower so that a comrade can more easily advance on a line of attack toward the objective. A more conventional use of the term is to protect oneself or another person against the elements, whatever they may be.

Most of us are smart enough to look at what lies before us so that we don't trip, or we know what's around the corner so that there are no surprises. We do it for our kids so that they don't get injured or for our partners so that they aren't harmed. But when it comes to the boss, we too often relax our guard because we assume the boss is self-sufficient; otherwise, he or she would ask for help.

In fact, bosses have so many things coming at them from all directions that they often don't see what's on the blind side. That's where you come in, whether it's intercepting an unwanted phone call or an uninvited visitor or stepping in when the conversation the boss is having with a client drifts into a caution zone.

There should be a business etiquette for such awkward situations, but there isn't. Actually, there should be internal ground rules or guardrails you can and should establish to provide yourself and your boss with that much-needed cover when the unexpected occurs.

Because I have engaged in literally thousands of interviews with reporters over the years, there should have been little surprise on my part in virtually any interview circumstance. Yet without a pre-determined policy for that unforgettable, irretrievable answer to a last-second, throwaway question, I found myself kicking myself for not protecting the boss from the unanticipated.

Reporters are a quirky bunch, each with a unique personality and a self-styled approach to the craft. One journalist I liked but found particularly hard to warm to was R. Jeffrey Smith of the *Washington Post*. Jeff covered the Pentagon like a blanket, ever present and forever inquiring about things other reporters didn't seem to care about or weren't aware of.

When in late April 1990 he paid me a visit to request an interview with General Powell, I asked him exactly what I asked every reporter requesting an interview with my boss: "What's the issue?" Just in general the state of the force at this point in his chairmanship was the answer. Fair enough; the public had a right to know the answer to what he was asking. Moreover, Jeff was a legitimate conduit to that public, especially a Washington-based public that included important stakeholders, not the least of which was Congress.

The chairman agreed to the interview with Smith, and they met in the general's office on May 3 in midafternoon. As usual, I prepared the general with likely questions and proposed answers. We sat, the three of us, for about 30 minutes, the typical amount of time we set aside for print interviews.

Jeff poked around with a series of questions, nothing earthshaking or groundbreaking. I had told him in advance he'd have a half hour to ask his questions. At the 28-minute mark I called for one last question. After the general's answer, we stood up and headed for the door. Halfway across the room, Jeff said, "Given this new 'peace dividend' everyone is talking about with the Soviet military shrinking, what do you see the size of our base force becoming?"

Ill prepared for this awkward moment and unanticipated last question, I said nothing. I had no cover for the boss such as "That's a weighty question deserving of a full response at a moment when we have more time" or something equally urbane. But no, not me.

Nothing in time to protect the boss before he waded into deep water with an acknowledgment that the threat was different. Smith pressed him on whether cuts in the size of the force were possible. Time for a hasty retreat on our part.

However, the general took the bait with a yes. Smith hooked him with a percentage he was looking at and reeled him in with his answer of 25 percent. Nice going, Smullen, who stood helpless and hopeless as the chairman made news—big news! The story was on the front pages the next Monday. Congressional Democrats loved it: a money saver. The boss's boss, Secretary Dick Cheney, was not nearly as pleased; he hadn't been consulted. Never surprise the boss by letting him or her learn about it for the first time by reading it, whatever the "it" is, in the morning paper. Makes for a bad start to the day. When the reports of potential force reductions reached Europe a day later, NATO allies complained that they hadn't been warned.

How's that for a perfect storm? And to think we had almost made it out the door with Jeff Smith in tow before he caught us standing and napping. This was not the first time a reporter had attempted the "throwaway" last question or the "bait and switch" whereby he or she says the interview is about X but turns it to Y.

The lesson of that day is seared in my mind. Other attempts by other reporters have since been tried on me, but never again did they get the same result. To begin with, I have an obligation to the boss to prepare him for the inevitable but also for the unexpected. Further, I have a responsibility to keep the train on the track with respect to where the conversation goes.

It's a "Jack be nimble, Jack be quick" approach to providing cover for the boss: anticipating where the land mines are and maneuvering through or around them, having a game plan that is flexible and responsive to anything that might come up.

Have a policy that allows for your intervention if something is asked that deserves a "wait, out" answer. Or step in with the right answer if the boss gets it wrong or only half right. Inserting yourself into the conversation or taking a protective position takes the boss off the hook. If nothing else, it gives the boss time to think of an acceptable answer or a policy he or she can live with.

This is not about throwing yourself in front of the boss to shield the boss. It's about providing the boss some cover as he or she homes in on the objective of providing the best answer. The boss will be grateful; you'll be purposeful. Great combination.

38

Assume Someone's
Always Watching

Teaching the principles of life begins early, as I saw firsthand while walking through the corridors of an elementary school in Fabius, New York, not long ago. Above the hallway was a large sign that simply said, "Character: what you say or do when no one else is looking."

Simple words but so important for young ones to know. As we grow older, there are more people in our lives who watch our every move. A corollary of that definition of character is that "someone is always watching what you say or do." That implies that you should be the best you can be at everything you do.

That is particularly important for all of us who take pride in any group of which we are a part: a corporation, an institution, a nonprofit organization. Our actions should reflect that pride. We should believe in it, what it stands for, and what it can accomplish. If we don't, we're probably in the wrong place in life.

Having been in military service for 20 years in 1983, I had come to love my army. I was fiercely defensive of it, full of pride in it. Peril can accompany either of these positions, as I discovered.

Such was the case in the aftermath of the October 25, 1983, U.S.-led invasion of Grenada. A Caribbean island nation with a population at the time of about 100,000 situated 100 miles north of Venezuela, it had both a Cuban and a Soviet presence ashore.

Code-named Operation Urgent Fury, the invasion was triggered by a bloody military coup conducted by a party faction. The
uprising was led by Deputy Prime Minister Bernard Coard, who
seized power and murdered Prime Minister Maurice Bishop. The
Organization of American States appealed to the United States for
assistance in response to the political instability.

In light of the island's proximity to the United States as well
as a presence on the island at the time of U.S. medical students at
St. George's University, President Reagan chose to take military
action. He called on the U.S. Army's Rapid Deployment Force,
consisting of two Ranger battalions and 82nd Airborne Division
paratroopers, along with Marines, Army Delta Force personnel,
and Navy SEALs. In all, 7,600 troops from the United States,
Jamaica, and the Regional Security System quickly defeated the
Grenadian resistance forces and rescued the students.

All's well that ends well. Or so it seemed until a year later, when
Bill Keller, an up-and-coming reporter for the *New York Times*
and later its managing editor, wrote a special story in the Sunday,
October 6, edition of that paper. It was critical of the various U.S.
military services for being quarrelsome factions competing for
money while "tripping over one another in battle." Two extremely
powerful senators, Barry Goldwater, Republican of Arizona, and
Sam Nunn, Democrat of Georgia, leveled assaults on the U.S. military for the way the services were run.

Citing speeches both of these members of the Senate Armed
Services Committee had given, Keller referred specifically to the
Grenada invasion a year earlier as an example of quarrels and mis-
communication among the military services. In one speech, Keller
cited Senator Nunn as having described how an army officer in the
Grenada invasion was forced to use his American Telephone and
Telegraph (AT&T) credit card from a phone booth on the beach
where he had landed to call his office in North Carolina. "The
officer," said Nunn, "was seeking to coordinate navy air support
for his troops because army units on the ground and the navy's
shipboard command post had incompatible radios."

When I read the story the next day, it just didn't sound right. As the chief of media relations for the U.S. Army at the time and always interested in the facts of this or any army matter, I put one of my assistants on the case. He returned from the bowels of the Pentagon later that day with zero evidence that the story was true.

A few days went by during which the AT&T credit card story gained traction. Print and broadcast reports about the incident appeared in numerous places. My boss, the chief of army public affairs, asked what I knew about those stories. I assured him we had run them to ground. Yes, it was good theater in written form, but in actuality it had not happened.

Keller came wandering into my office later in the week asking if I'd comment on the reports of the army having to resort to a personal AT&T credit card because radios between services were incompatible. Not true, I told him; simply didn't happen.

By then the story had become a factoid, told so many times by so many people that it became fact in the minds of most. Keller couldn't wait to report to Sam Nunn that an army colonel in the Pentagon—that would be me—had questioned the senator's story.

A reaction came quickly. Two senior officers from the army's Legislative Liaison Office appeared in my office the next day. "You are in deep trouble," one of them said. "Senator Nunn does not appreciate being called a liar," the other said. He wanted an apology and a retraction of my position that the incident hadn't occurred, they breathlessly told me.

The furor drifted up to the secretary of the army's office. Secretary Marsh, a former member of Congress, calmly asked me what I knew about the Grenada telephone credit card call story. Checked and double-checked, I assured him. He asked the army staff to verify my side of the story, and they did. Word got back to Senator Nunn that the army stood by its position.

Two days later, I learned that several special operations officers involved in the invasion were summoned to Washington to personally meet with Senator Nunn to recount what had actually happened. It did not involve an AT&T credit card, they told him.

Apparently, my career was salvaged and my hide was safe. Never heard another word. Yet the story lives on in military circles to this day. It's simply too dramatic, juicy, and controversial to die.

However, the fact that somebody's always watching will never die, at least in my mind. Everything you say, everything you do, whether personally or professionally, is subject to scrutiny. That goes for your boss, too. Keep a watch out for the boss. In this age of transparency, every word or action needs to stand the accountability test.

Don't shy away from whatever it takes to get the job done for your boss or the company for which you work. Be willing to push the envelope as long as you know you're right and can stand behind what you say or do. If I had not done that in the case of the AT&T credit card story, it probably would have made it to movie theaters somewhere along the way. Sorry, Hollywood.

39

Life Is Not a Spectator Sport

"Life is just one damned thing after another." So said nineteenth-century American editor, publisher, and writer Elbert Hubbard. He didn't differentiate between the personal and professional sides of life, but either way he was right. We're a busy people, more so today than when he wrote those true words.

The way we spend time professionally is a function of what kind of job we have, demands on us in our job, and whether we control our destiny each day. We probably do better than the boss, who has to respond to more demands. Does anyone help the boss manage that schedule, sort out his or her requirements, and point the conductor of the organizational train to the right stations, helping the boss make the right stops? Someone should, even if it's not requested of that person.

Far too often, the leader gets so wrapped up in meetings and spending time with visitors that he or she misses what is happening outside the immediate circle of office life. Widen that circle if you can and, if the boss will let you, try to mix the activities he or she engages in.

When was the last time your boss left the office to be with the employees in another part of the building or in another facility? Has the boss recently walked the workplace floor, visited the assembly line, had lunch in the cafeteria with employees, or stopped by a watercooler or communal coffee bar to chat with folks? If the boss

157

does these kinds of things, does he or she do them without a lot of physical presence of the staff? The boss can take mental notes; no need for a note taker. And watch the look on people's faces.

Another way to see what is outside the boss's comfort zone is to have the boss look for opportunities to meet stakeholders he or she might not normally see: family members, retirees, vendors, customers, government officials, elected officials, area residents, anyone who has a vested interest in the organization and how it's run.

After the Gulf War in 1991—43 days total, 100 hours for the ground campaign—when we routed Saddam Hussein's army, there was an overwhelming outpouring of public appreciation. Great praise was given to the servicemen and servicewomen who accomplished that remarkable operational feat.

Thanks came in many forms. Major League Baseball was just beginning the 1991 season, and teams found ways to express their appreciation. The New York Yankees wanted a chance to pay their respects. I took their telephonic invitation for General Colin Powell to throw out the first pitch at a game in Yankee Stadium on April 15, 1991.

The chairman wasn't very interested; there was lots going on. True, but here was a chance for him to receive a tribute on behalf of the "troops" who had performed so well in battle, all 541,000 of them. This ceremonial salute would be seen in person by nearly 58,000 in the ballpark, by millions watching the game on television, and by tens of millions who would see the press reports later on TV and in newspapers.

You can't buy that kind of publicity, I suggested. He agreed. We accepted. That was the easy part. The hard part was getting him focused and ready to "throw it down the pike." On the Friday before the Monday game, I rode home with him at the end of the day to his quarters. "How about a little practice throwing a baseball this weekend?" I suggested. "Don't need any," he replied. I reminded him that President George H. W. Bush had thrown the first pitch days earlier at the Texas Rangers opener low and into the dirt in front of home plate. "I'll be just fine," the general said as he climbed out of the sedan.

All weekend I fretted over what might happen. In the dirt, over the catcher's head, way off to the side, all the way to the backstop. Yes, this was a spectator sport, but not when you're on the field and on television.

Off we went to New York City, to Yankee Stadium, the Mecca of professional baseball, situated in the Bronx, which happened to be the general's boyhood neighborhood. We spent time in the locker room with members of the Yankees. Great fun! We stood poised in the dugout along with Mayor David Dinkins. Great honor! The appointed hour and moment were upon us.

The chairman of the Joint Chiefs of Staff took the mound. My throat went dry as photographers lined up for the ceremonial first pitch. My eyes wanted to close but were bolted open. A cross between fear and anxiety gripped me.

Dressed in his utility military uniform, the chairman glanced at the catcher, who was crouched at home plate. He wound up and threw the ball fast and hard. Smack! A perfect strike into the catcher's mitt. The crowd went wild. My reaction was a yelp of relief and joy. He'd done it!

Pride in him, pride in the Yankees for putting him on their ceremonial stage, and pride in this grand salute to the armed forces of the United States. A magical moment to be sure.

Later, I learned from the general's son, Michael, that the two had practiced Saturday and Sunday to get it right. Yes, he had done that. No spectator in that man! It reminded me of the army expression "train as you fight; fight as you train."

In any leader, in any organization, the C-suite is not the sole seat to occupy. It's out on the front lines, meeting and greeting the people who matter most—those who have a stake in the company. Those who invest—their time, their money, their hope, and their promise—in what you do.

40

Keep the Staff Informed About Requirements and Decisions

An intriguing book I read during my graduate studies was required for a sociology class I took as an elective. It was *The Territorial Imperative* by Robert Ardrey. It taught me a lot about the animal origins of property and their relationships to humans and nations. The pack mentality and the alpha syndrome are not unlike organizational life for the leaders and the led, I learned.

Controlling territory and sharing the resources in it are often a function of who's in charge. I've been in organizations that have been very protective of such things as who knows what and when and determines how it's conveyed. It doesn't always happen, but such organizations can be dysfunctional. Being protective of information can be petty; it can also be harmful. To whom? To the boss and to the people up and down the food chain.

Keeping people informed is important for any size and type of organization. If it isn't a secret or if it's not compartmentalized information, it should be transmitted as far, as wide, and as swiftly as possible. As our sixteenth president, Abraham Lincoln, once said, "Let the people know the facts and the country will be safe."

It can be done verbally, electronically, or in memo form—in any way that not only keeps people informed but lets them feel a part of what's going on.

People at all levels have this transmission capability, be it a COO, a senior vice president, a chief of staff, a special assistant, or a secretary. Information is golden, and the wealth needs to be shared.

In 1997 I was fortunate enough to become the chief of staff of America's Promise—The Alliance for Youth. Its purpose was clear: to put valuable resources into the lives of at-risk youth. However, as a start-up, it had no blueprint or model to serve as a guide. I got to make it up as I went along. As someone who would have to help run it, I wanted an organizational structure that made sense. I divided staff responsibilities into teams or divisions, as they were called, as the first order of business. Then came the hiring of qualified employees, providing them direction, and overseeing their activities.

As chairman of the organization, Colin Powell set the standard and expectations. A president was hired, and together that person and I issued assignments on a regular basis.

I'm not a big fan of meetings, so I didn't often call the staff together to issue edicts. Instead, I chose a technique that has been called management by walking around. Each day I would wander out onto the floor of the office space we occupied to ask questions of various staff members and ensure that they had the benefit of the chairman's and president's thinking. At the same time, I would solicit thoughts from as many of the 60 members of the staff as I came in contact with.

Open lines of communication allowed them to ask me questions and at the same time gave me the opportunity to keep them informed. It seemed to work. I encouraged interactive dialogue between team members so that everyone knew what everyone else on the team was doing. There is nothing worse than being caught by surprise. It not only short-circuits the decision-making process, it obstructs the management process.

The worst thing that can happen in this regard is that an employee picks up the morning newspaper and reads about someone or something that happened at the office that he or she hadn't previously known about. The reaction can range from hurt to outrage, from feeling left out to feeling unimportant.

This can be particularly harmful if a crisis has erupted and you learn about it from the news. Every organization has multiple stakeholders, and the most important of them all are the employees. There is nothing worse than being the last to know and the first to go. Not being told about it but being responsible to do something about it is simply unacceptable.

Those in the chain of command who know what's going on regarding requirements and decisions need to share it as far and as wide among the staff as possible. Yes, it's about territory, but it's also about building a winning team. If that territory is to be protected, it needs an all-hands defense.

Having trust and confidence in your staff members and keeping them informed is an important thing. Ignore it at your peril.

41

Help Disallow
Threatening Behavior

One of the most dysfunctional and disruptive things that can happen in the workplace is to be threatened in one's job: not physical threats but mental or psychological provocation, not bullying but badgering.

Threatened by whom? Could be by the boss, by a fellow worker, by a newcomer to the scene, or even by oneself.

Not only can this result in lost labor-hours because you're plotting ways to overcome the threatening behavior instead of doing your work, it can cause disharmony on the organizational team by throwing it into disarray.

Why would and how could the boss threaten an employee? Easy! The boss may not like or respect someone in his or her employ. Instead of firing that person, most likely because the boss doesn't have the necessary for-cause rationale, the boss simply makes life unbearable for that employee: everything from harangue to harassment, from ignoring that person to passing him or her by for a raise or a promotion.

There are ample ways to disincentivize or discourage an employee from wanting to come to work. If you're the one in charge, stop it! If you work for the one in charge and have the ability, you can serve the boss best by asking him or her to stop it. If the boss won't or doesn't, there may be grounds for filing a formal complaint by the perceived victim. That is not helpful for the folks in human resources or the legal department.

If you're threatened by a coworker old or new and the incident is unwanted or unprovoked, talk to your boss about it. If that yields nothing, the filing of a formal grievance may be justified and appropriate. If you are threatened because of the old territorial imperative, you have choices. You can talk to your supervisor about being uncomfortable with having your space invaded if certain actions taken by someone are disruptive. If it's about jealousy more than anything else, you can talk to yourself about getting over it and on with it.

People do not want to admit they personally are the problem, but there are elements of insecurity in all of us. As the late *New York Times* editor and reporter James Kilpatrick once said, "Realities count, but images often count for more."

Life isn't always as it seems; much of what we hear and see is distortion brought on by the filters we allow to operate in our brains. Can't see it, don't believe it, won't accept it! If you think the boss is favoring the new employee with obvious attention to that person and not to you, it may be for a reason. If there is no justifiable reason, have the courage to ask for a discussion with the boss, who may not have a clue that there's a problem. But first have a conversation with yourself.

I've witnessed many real or perceived threats to people's workplace livelihoods or their fragile personalities. Some were perception-fed; others were realities.

In one personal instance, I unwittingly yet unintentionally caused the problem. Upon assuming a new position of supervisory responsibility in one particular job change, I gave more assignments to one assistant than to her counterpart. They were of equal rank but not in terms of the attention I gave to one over the other because of her more valued skill set.

Unaware that there was resentment by the one who felt shunned, I continued to call for the other to do more because she thrived on what I gave her and was good at it. I eventually encountered the penalty: the employee who felt left out quit and took a position elsewhere. With her departure went years of institutional memory that was difficult to replace. My fault!

In another instance, I was asked by a friend to lend a hand during an institutional crisis he was experiencing. Overburdened by the responses to and requirements of the crisis, he called and asked me to come in person to help him. I agreed to pitch in with strategic advice and counsel.

To avoid threatening either the communications or the legislative talent he had in-house, I met with the heads of both of those departments. I told them I was there only temporarily to be on call to help in any way at any time. My advice was provided pro bono, and my offer of intended help was honorable.

They welcomed my mostly long-distance, occasionally in-person involvement. My goal was not to interfere but to help their respective teams. They never felt threatened and quite frankly appreciated the extra hand.

To threaten someone else in the workplace is unacceptable behavior. To feel threatened at work by someone else is uncomfortable but resolvable. It can be fixed with the help of others who want to serve the boss best. To be in a position of leadership and allow it is inexcusable. To be silent is sad; to be obstinate is unhelpful. Get to the bottom of the problem by speaking out, by putting your best foot forward, by finding a solution for both or all parties.

I can't recall one situation in which allowing threatening behavior in the office led to a positive outcome. Lost labor-hours and sleep are irretrievable. If your job expectations are not being met, ask to have a discussion with your immediate supervisor. If that fails to result in a more acceptable work environment, it may be time for a move—over to a new department or position or onward and outward to a new employer.

There's nothing worse than not wanting to head out the door in the morning to an unpleasant atmosphere in the office. There is a solution somewhere—find it and fix it. You'll be serving the organization, the boss, and yourself by doing so.

42

Don't Be Afraid to Take a Risk

Risk can be a frightening or an exhilarating experience. You can run from it because you fear it or gravitate toward it because you seek the thrill or excitement of something unique.

Most people are risk-averse. They answer affirmatively to Alfred E. Neuman's "What, me worry?" question. In contrast, there are hurricane hunters, cliff climbers, and high-wire walkers who think nothing about beating the odds of taking a chance.

Having jumped out of airplanes, I tend to relate to those willing to take a chance, a walk on the wild side if you will. It's not for the faint of heart; if one is drawn to a moment of uncertainty and it excites that person, so be it. The payoff can be grand.

Fortunately, in the everyday world of doing business, calamities are not waiting around every corner. However, there are opportunities to improve on the outcome of an event or a cause by taking unusual, even risk-laden steps to achieve a goal.

Scientists devise formulas to determine the probability of success or failure of an experiment. Others rely more on faith in hard work and intuition. That doesn't suggest just bumbling along hoping for the best. It's more about designing the best strategic plan based on the most thoughtful considerations.

Back in 1989, I was part of a historic and unprecedented event. My boss, Admiral William J. Crowe, Jr., the eleventh chairman of the Joint Chiefs of Staff, was invited by his Soviet counterpart to visit the USSR. For nearly 45 years the Soviet Union and the United States had faced off on opposite sides of the so-called Iron Curtain. They were two superpowers poised to do mortal combat the outcome of which could have led to Armageddon.

Crowe had asked his former counterpart, Marshal Sergei Akhromeyev, to visit him in the United States in 1988. That in itself was a daring act; inviting the known enemy into your tent was considered a bit risky. However, the admiral, a kind and cunning man, exposed the wary but curious Soviet leader to the beauty and principled nature of our society and its people. Come see this thing we call a democracy, Crowe beckoned, in hopes of building trust.

Turnabout is fair play. Come see this thing we call a communist state, the Soviets countered a year later. We couldn't wait to see firsthand this thing we called and believed to be a Russian bear, 12 feet tall at least. Or was it? The invitation from Akhromeyev's successor, General Mikhail Moiseyev, was to spend 11 days and cross 11 time zones to see, touch, and feel the proverbial beast.

World-class stuff, this moment in time. How were we going to share it with the American people? the admiral asked me in April, 60 days or so before the planned trip. Or should we not attempt to document it at all, given the uncertain nature of the outcome? It could be a bust.

Too historic a moment, was my response. We needed to capture it somehow, and the best way to do that was through the eyes and ears of the press in some form or another. Should we take a pool of reporters with us or simply rely on those who would be on Soviet soil watching our every move?

He and I were alone in his Pentagon office debating the pros and cons, the risks and ramifications involved. The chairman was not risk-averse, and neither was I. We opted for a high-stakes approach: one news organization to capture it all as part of our travel party to the Soviet Union. We settled on the late Mike Wallace of *60 Minutes*. Risk aplenty. Wallace was known as one of the best but toughest American broadcast journalists; CBS's *60 Minutes* was a highly-regarded program known for its thorough, thoughtful reporting. Often, however, they were critical of the U.S. military about everything from bad decisions to faulty weapons systems.

Why risk asking *60 Minutes*? The knowns were several. Wallace had covered the Akhromeyev visit in 1988; he and the admiral had hit it off well. He described himself as "tough but fair," and he was. *60 Minutes* was one of the most respected programs on American television, with a demographic audience that would fall into the intelligentsia category.

The unknowns were several as well. There was no guarantee the Soviets would allow Wallace and his crew to accompany us to record our every move in their country. Moreover, there was no assurance that the story that would come of this, even if they agreed, would favor either the Soviets or us. Yet the admiral and I concluded that we'd never get a second chance to make a first impression.

We pressed forward to gain the Soviets' permission. Haltingly they agreed after the exchange of dozens of cables on the matter. They countered our request for acceptance with their demand for certain security conditions, to which we agreed. Next came my overture to Mike Wallace to accompany us but to agree to play by Soviet rules. When I called to ask if he would have an interest in joining such a venture into the unknown, he jumped at the invitation and the chance to be a witness to history.

Lots of planning took place before our departure. Wallace agreed to meet us in Helsinki, Finland, the Sunday before our Monday, June 13, departure for Moscow. Our official travel party numbered fewer than 20, plus the *60 Minutes* crew, which consisted of Wallace; his producer, Barry Lando; a cameraman; and a sound-light technician. As a group, we gathered for a predeparture dinner in the hotel on Sunday night. I felt like offering a prayer that this venture would turn out well but thought better of it. Silently I said it on my own.

Early the next day we were off to Moscow on what I sensed would be an excellent adventure. Wallace interviewed Crowe en route, asking him on camera what he anticipated and hoped to achieve. The admiral allowed that he wasn't sure of the outcome but knew it was a seminal moment.

Like a first dance, it was a bit strained and awkward at the beginning, with most of the attention on the visitors from America. With more than a bit of actor in him, the admiral knew he was on the world stage. Always comfortable in his own skin, he became a showman starting with the opening act, an interview upon arrival on the tarmac of the international airport in the Soviet capital. He subsequently was interviewed by reporters at every stop, in every setting, by anyone who wanted to ask what he had seen, what he felt about it, and what he sensed it meant.

Along the way, as often as possible, he sat with Mike Wallace one-on-one. Wallace and Lando were beside themselves with the access they had. Both of them handled it in the most professional way.

Unlike Crowe, the head of the Soviet general staff wanted nothing to do with the press. Moiseyev would position himself outside the circle of reporters who were assembled at each stop to ask questions of the admiral. I asked my Soviet counterpart why Moiseyev didn't participate in those media availability sessions. "The general does not do interviews," was his brusque answer. A model of risk aversion.

On the second day, while visiting a Soviet air base, I mentioned this to the admiral, who whispered, "Watch." Midway through a barrage of questions being flung his way, Crowe paused, motioned to General Moiseyev to join him for the questioning, and waited until the Russian hesitatingly entered the circle. Behavior modification at its best. Uncomfortable at first with the spotlight on him, Moiseyev eventually eased into his new interviewee role.

Tellingly, by the fourth day, he and the admiral were fighting for a position of attention both literally and figuratively. They both realized the world was watching and listening courtesy of the reporters from around the globe who were on the scene covering a piece of history.

Over the course of 11 days, the *60 Minutes* crew shot massive amounts of video. They captured our visits to many military installations, rides aboard helicopters, trips at sea on a guided missile frigate, a tour of a submarine in the Barents Sea. We even got a close-up view of a Soviet nuclear missile site. There were stops at monuments and museums, talks with Russian veterans of World War II, and best of all talks with the common citizens of the many cities we visited. No holds barred, virtually no restrictions. Only once did they ask me to have Mike Wallace shut off the camera at a highly classified site. He quickly did.

When we said our goodbyes in Vladivostok on our last evening in that immense country we had seen end to end, inside and out, we had mixed emotions. We were sad to end our adventure with new friends we once thought were the enemy but happy to be climbing aboard that shiny blue and white air force jet with the words *United States of America* adorning both sides.

Once airborne, the admiral called a group of us up to his cabin. Some sat at the conference table and others were on the floor, all of us tired but content to be going home. The chairman asked us the question of the day, perhaps the century. "What do you make of what we did and saw these past 11 days?" he asked. Sounding like a bunch of amateur philosophers, some of us took turns at suggesting what this had meant and would be likely to mean over time. None of us got it quite right, but collectively we believed something different yet important in the life of the U.S.-Soviet relationship was occurring. And looking back, it was; it was the beginning of the end of the Cold War.

What if we hadn't allowed this historic event to be documented courtesy of *60 Minutes*? Sure, it still would have happened, and it would have been covered intermittently by countless reporters. But the sights and the sounds, the nuances and notions that played out consistently each day would have been lost. Yes, we took a chance that it would turn out to be a positive experience. When Mike Wallace rendered a 15-minute report on *60 Minutes* in early September, it was better than just plain good. It was an incredible account of how the world was changing, he concluded, for the better.

Not everyone gets to take such rides and risks; not everyone wants to. At the same time, all of us should want to put forth the best image and account of our people, our products, our services, and our stakeholders. To get to do it successfully with competence and confidence is a rewarding thing. To not want to do it because something could go wrong along the way will yield little more than another day, another dollar.

The latter is not my idea of gain. There is no chance of true prosperity in such an approach. Risk is not about being a good gambler. It's more about being a good manager of opportunities that can lead to measurable successes for you, your boss, and the things you stand for and can stand behind. Relax, Alfred.

43

Build and Maintain Relationships

For sure, money and material resources are important in life. They sustain us and improve our position on the ladder of life. But make no mistake: people are the most important thing in life to us humans; strong, lasting relationships with people are things money can't buy.

As Charles Darwin told us in his book *The Expression of the Emotions in Man and Animals*, published in 1872, humans need to work on emotional expression to survive and adapt. In the workplace that theory extends to understanding and managing people for whom you are responsible: those above, below, and around you.

As you navigate the social environment of the workplace you occupy, you can be the helmsman and steer the day so that it will turn out well. A good way to start is to check your negative emotions at the door. Put on your game face and take the pulse of the emotions of others. Harness the negative ones; set free the positive kind.

It starts with self-awareness of your moods and a sense of the moods of those around you. If yours are not in check, it may be because of a concern or dilemma or abnormal condition at home or on the private side of life. If that is the case, you need to find the inner strength to table it until you can dedicate your time and energy to fix whatever it is that's bothering you.

Can't do it, you say? Then try what I call compartmentalization. Park whatever it is that is adversely affecting you at least temporarily. Put it away in the recesses of your mind until the time is right to pull that "it" out for the sake of resolution.

If others around you are in an emotionally bad place, work at sensing, understanding, and reacting to their being out of sync. That can be as easy as giving them a pat on the back, conveying a friendly word, or having a helpful chat to help them regain their balance. It can inspire and influence their ability to accomplish more than would otherwise be possible.

If you can translate that into treating every day as game day, you will help bring people together to complete the assigned tasks. The results can be a function of having done things well or not.

As someone responsible for results, build a reputation for being good at organizing and coordinating those activities for which you're responsible. Be able to delegate responsibilities to others; recognize that you can't do it all. Be good at organizing people, ideas, and resources. Be adept at strategic planning and implementation.

Peering into the C-suite, you may see that the boss needs your emotional support more than anyone else on the team. What if the boss is in less than an admirable emotional state? If you are in a position of influence, you might choose to determine the source of the problem. What triggered it? and What is an appropriate reaction to it? are questions I would ask.

Soon after taking a new job position, I was asked to sit in on a budget meeting. At the table were my boss, the finance representative, a coworker, and me. I was new to the game but not to the boss. I came to see my boss in a different light this particular day. He was clearly having a bad hair day. He asked tough questions. He drilled down on detail. He expected very specific and favorable answers to his questions.

The keeper of the coin described new accounting procedures required of her to keep the books. They were not easy to reconcile, she said. The boss chose not to recognize or accept the new procedures or their difficulty. He didn't like them, and furthermore, he rejected some of her answers to his pointed questions.

Finally he erupted. He lashed out at her. He screamed at her. He belittled her. As an observer, I was most uncomfortable. Near tears, she struggled through the tongue-lashing. The boss sensed her frustration and hurt. He fortunately adjourned the meeting before she experienced total meltdown.

Later, I sought her out. I apologized on his behalf and told her to keep on doing what was right to perform her job well and properly. It was a private but important moment for her. It helped restore her confidence. It helped me build a better understanding of how to handle a similar situation if it occurred again. I later suggested to the boss that he had been tougher than he had to be on his fiduciary counsel. I wasn't sure if his nod meant he agreed or he was trying to downplay the moment.

Managing others well in the workplace is a gift that is learned and a skill that is honed. It starts with understanding others, listening to them, educating them, or even accepting their advice.

It starts with building strong relationships with your teammates. That can come best by offering hope and incentives for those who work for you. It comes from offering support and assistance for those with whom you work. It comes by offering your best advice and counsel to the boss about the importance of the people in his or her organization. That is priceless advice you owe the boss.

44

Every Problem Needs a Solution

No matter where you reside on the organizational ladder, you are going to confront problems. They're inevitable and merit a double reaction—to accept them and to do something about them.

Forget about the past and what could or should have been. It's too late now. Sure, learn from what happened or went wrong so that you don't repeat it, but invest not in feeling helpless or defeated but in moving things to a better place.

The most efficient way around an obstacle or problem is to recognize a way, the best way, forward. Sometimes that takes courage or creativity, but it also takes persistence to overcome whatever has occurred.

It could be a management mistake or a leadership shortcoming. It could be poor business performance or a bad financial decision. It could be a fraudulent action or even a failing business endeavor. Whether political, economical, or managerial, the problem needs a solution.

Once you've identified the problem, define its seriousness and impact. Formulate a strategy to resist or reverse the dilemma. Allocate resources to apply to the wound. Administer thoughtful actions that can serve as a surgical solution. Allow time for the healing and evaluate the results to ensure that there has been a cure.

Sometimes you may have a problem that you never saw coming. When General Powell formed America's Promise in 1997, we felt it was a benevolent cause. Putting helpful resources into the lives of the 15 million at-risk American youth seemed like a caring, responsible thing to do. It was an "if we are needed, we are there" response to a societal cancer that was spreading.

We assembled a staff and set them on various missions to create partnerships with both for-profit and not-for-profit organizations. Those collaborations stirred commitments to raise the level of people, spaces, money, healthcare, classrooms, and services for children at risk. With Colin Powell making the ask, the willingness to give to the cause came in the form of an impactful movement by America's Promise on behalf of at-risk kids.

Little did we realize we had stirred up a hornet's nest. Not all but some nonprofit organizations, many of which had been in existence for decades, felt threatened. We had infiltrated their territory and caused some of them to feel under siege.

As his chief of staff, I came in daily contact with nonprofit leaders, some of whom seemed wary of us. They didn't come out and say it directly, but I sensed their concern with our very existence. The not-for-profit world directed toward serving at-risk children is not so large that we couldn't sense a credibility problem by the very reaction of some to our existence.

Finally, I went to the general, who as chairman of America's Promise needed to know we had a perception problem. We discussed how to calm the nerves of the nonprofit community leaders who felt we had invaded their turf.

What to do? We recognized we had a problem; it was more perception than reality but a problem nevertheless. We were committed to act in a way that would resolve the problem. We realized we needed to build bridges to create a culture of collaboration and cooperation, not competition and conflict.

We arrived at a strategy. It was to look other nonprofits in the eye, so to speak, and through face-to-face discussions allow them to air their concerns. We hoped to negotiate a settlement to the perceived problem and convince them that we harbored no ill will or desire to take or steal anything or anyone they felt was their due.

With the help of a nonprofit colleague who knew the community well and knew those who felt threatened we set a date and place that seemed neutral enough, the Salvation Army headquarters in Alexandria, Virginia, to convene a meeting. We invited one and all nonprofit leaders to come and hear our motives for helping children, discuss their concerns about how that might interfere with their missions to do the same thing, and determine how we might resolve those issues that were in contention.

It was a midmorning to midafternoon affair. The general spoke his piece first, which was designed to be conciliatory. Many others in response expressed their views as well. Frank, open discussion prevailed. At the end of the session, we had seemingly assuaged any concerns that had preexisted. We let them know we did not want what rightfully belonged to them. Rather, we wanted to be a partner and a friend. It's amazing how healthy dialogue can lead to helpful relationships.

When all was said and done, we had engaged in a problem-solving process that worked for us and can work for others as well. It starts with recognizing the problem, identifying the issue or issues involved, and being committed to a valid solution.

Solutions are the hardest part. Understanding the interests of everyone involved sets you on a path of determining the problem-solving options available to you. Evaluate each one, weighing the merits and demerits. Select the best option available and agree to monitor and evaluate the progress being made.

If you are ever in a position to identify a problem, you can ignore it or do something about it. If it's smoldering, you have time to be a bit more deliberate than you do if it's a raging inferno.

Either way, you have an obligation to the boss, actually two obligations. First, you need to let him or her know there's a problem. Second and more important, you need to come armed with a proposed solution to whatever the threat might be. Otherwise you become part of the problem yourself.

45

Build a Comfort Zone
for the Boss

The term *comfort zone* is used more often than not to describe a behavioral range within which a person operates. Sometimes it's used to define a place a person is either in or out of.

You might be described as being out of your comfort zone, for example, when you are going to the dentist for a root canal, sitting in the front seat of a roller coaster scared out of your wits, or skydiving from an airplane for the first time. Typically a heightened sense of anxiety is involved.

Being in a comfort zone is an anxiety-neutral condition in which there is no risk and your behavioral state allows you to deliver a steady and confident level of performance. There is no argument about which is better; being in the comfort zone is preferable.

Highly successful people actively seek their comfort zone so that their performance is enhanced or even optimized. If this is accomplished routinely or over an extended period, a higher level of skill or performance can be achieved.

Most professionals, including bosses, don't necessarily consider themselves in any particular comfort zone. They simply do what they do because it's expected—when, in fact, those of us who have responsibility for managing the boss ought to be seeking new and higher-level comfort zones on the boss's behalf. We should help take our bosses to places to which they're unaccustomed but in which they can experience greater organizational success. Think of it as an optimum performance level or a comfort zone in waiting.

Admiral Crowe had been chairman of the Joint Chiefs for three years when he inherited me as his public affairs advisor. The day I assumed that job, I gathered my staff of six. That was not a large number for the task of providing good counsel to the nation's top military man, but they were all cream-of-the-crop practitioners.

Knowing that the admiral would be taking a 22-day trip to five nations in the Far East in just two weeks, I asked my staff what public events the chairman usually engaged in when overseas. Only ceremonial events, was the answer. What, no public speeches to noteworthy forums, no joint press conferences with his military counterparts, no one-on-one interviews with key reporters in the region, no media availabilities along the way?

No, none of those things, was their answer. "Why not?" I asked. Simple; he had never been asked, they responded.

A man comfortable in his own skin, the admiral did not shrink from public attention. Therefore, in a memo to him the next day, I challenged him to a number of public, media-driven activities during the upcoming trip. I assured him I would take responsibility for the actions and would gain concurrence from the U.S. ambassadors in the countries we were to visit. The admiral readily agreed to the proposal.

The burden was now on me to assemble a comfort zone that was acceptable, well designed, and well supported, and I did. With him every step of the way on the trip, I managed his engagement in several public events in the form of speeches, joint press conferences, and interviews. Stressing the importance of strong bilateral relations with the nations of Singapore, Thailand, Australia, the Philippines, and Japan, he mesmerized audiences with U.S. public outreach in the region. On a personal level, the successes he attained served as a solid foundation for my relationship with the admiral. They led to his willingness, even eagerness, to engage in subsequent bilateral activities during his last year in office before retirement.

In terms of performance management and development, the increase in public events and activities caused him to enter a new and acceptable comfort zone. Willing to explore new venues, he met with success after success, making his last year as chairman a period of optimal attention and achievement both at home and abroad. His public image went sky high.

Sure, there was more than a touch of luck involved, but taking the boss to a higher level was also a function of strategic thinking and planning. In Crowe's case, knowing the audiences and publics he could reach, thinking of global messages that resonated with those publics, and having a vision for how that would leave lasting impressions with stakeholders all contributed to the desired outcome: building a better, stronger U.S. brand.

If you assume your boss has a brand—and he or she does—find ways to take the boss to places he or she has never been or thought to go. If the boss is stuck in a comfort zone that is limiting, devise a plan for raising the level of involvement or engagement. Take forward your ideas for how to do that in steps that are achievable. Be convincing with your initiative to move the boss forward.

Accept that there may be reluctance or even a fear to wander into the unknown or new territory. If the boss is willing to try it on for size, it just might fit and become a habit. Measure the differences the boss has made and evaluate the successes he or she has achieved. Being bold is not bad; in fact, it can feel good for the boss and be good for business.

46

It's the Deed,
Not the Credit

In any organization, large or small, there are a lot of people who seek attention, need praise, or require credit for what they do. For some, the credit part is especially important before performance reviews or promotion periods.

It's human nature to want to be thought well of, to be remembered for things one does, to get a pat on the back when it's deserved. That's all well and good, but wouldn't it be so much better if people did their jobs not so much for credit but for accomplishment? Sure, recognition in life is important, but so is getting the job done well because that too is important.

While I was sitting at my desk in my seventh-floor State Department office in August 2001, my assistant told me I had a visitor. It was one of the senior members of the department's Bureau of Diplomatic Security (DS) unit. This was a team of federal agents whose job it was to provide protection for the secretary of state and other members of the diplomatic corps, both foreign and domestic.

He had come to ask for my assistance in arranging for a request that had come from the Make-A-Wish Foundation. He was hoping that as the chief of staff for the department and the secretary, I might have some power to influence the situation. The real power was the inspiration this incredible busy group of security agents provided. They routinely protected the secretary yet found time to nurture a relationship they had built with Make-A-Wish.

The agent told me that on behalf of a young lad, Brendan Kelly, from Great Falls, Virginia, the foundation had an important request. Four-year-old Brendan had a life-threatening illness, leukemia. He had but one wish. He had told the foundation, "I wish to meet the Pope." They had offered him a trip to Disney World, a meeting with Cal Ripken of the Baltimore Orioles, and other amazing opportunities. Brendan's request was simple: "I want to meet the Pope." Could I help? the agent asked. Let me work on it, I told him.

The United States has embassies all over the world. One of them is in the Vatican. It just so happened that I knew the recently sworn-in ambassador to the Holy See, Jim Nicholson. I messaged him and asked if he would intervene. Time went by, and with that grew uncertainty about whether a miracle was possible. Finally, word came back that Pope John Paul II would grant Brendan his wish.

I had been working by phone with a Make-A-Wish coordinator. I called him to give him the agreed-to date and meeting time with the Pope. He called Brendan's parents, and they said they'd make it.

The once-in-a-lifetime opportunity took place in the Pope's private chapel in early September. Afterward, when the foundation coordinator called to tell me the wish was complete, he mentioned that on the day the Kelly family was to depart for Rome, Brendan's parents couldn't find him in his bedroom or elsewhere in the house. Their search for him led outside, where they found him still in his pajamas sitting next to the family car holding his teddy bear. He didn't want to be late for the trip.

I conveyed to the DS detail that the wish had been fulfilled. I complimented them on their initiative. But this was not about credit as much as it was about the deed. The 81-year-old pontiff had made Brendan's day, and the satisfaction from that happening made mine as well.

In managing people I have always found and taken the time to say thank you for a job well done. That is an important cultural tradition that one should adopt in one's professional life. Give credit where credit is due. But don't build into the praise the expectation that it is required. The ideal working atmosphere is one in which employees do what needs to be done for the boss, the brand, and the organization. All will reap the benefits.

Wouldn't it be a better world if each morning as we looked in the mirror to brush our teeth, comb our hair, or check our attire, we said to ourselves, "I'm going to do something good and worthwhile today." You may not know what that will be, but what a good goal you have set for yourself.

Then, at the end of the day as you looked into that mirror, what a sense of satisfaction you would have if you could honestly say, "I did what I set out to do today." It wouldn't make for a perfect world, but it would make for a better world. It really is about the deed, not the credit for having accomplished something.

In the case of helping with the Make-A-Wish request to fulfill Brendan's wish to see the Pope, I can't recall even sharing the deed with the secretary of state. I was doing it as much for the reputation of the State Department as for him. That was something he would have naturally expected out of his team.

47

Be a Conscience for Your Boss

It is no surprise that the boss cannot be everywhere at work, whether it's at one moment in time or all the time. It therefore helps if the boss has the eyes and ears of others to depend on. Not to serve as spies or alarms but to be trusted agents who can honestly and reliably measure the good and the bad in and around the workplace for the boss.

That can range from determining attitudes of employees to measuring the quality of the work being done. It can also mean sensing when something is broken or wrong.

You may never be asked to be a lookout for or a gauge of things happening. Yet if you are in a position of responsibility within an organization, it's not only okay to be a conscience, it's almost a duty.

That doesn't have to be every day. That doesn't have to be in every way. But it should be whenever you can or wherever you go to see, listen, and learn on behalf of the boss.

I put this in the category of passionate curiosity, wanting to take the pulse of the organization for the good of the organization. It's about having mental inquisitiveness about the people who work here, the facility in which we work, the infrastructure that holds that facility together, the technology we use, the products we build, the services we provide, and the profits we make.

It may be as innocent as going to the cafeteria for lunch. Sitting with friends is fine. Sitting with a stranger can be even finer. I've known senior leaders who think going to the cafeteria to be seen is cool. They are seen by the unwashed masses to be sure, but when they bring with them their staff with whom they sit and talk, it is far from impressive.

As chief of staff of the State Department, I would routinely wander about the Main State Building to meet and talk with members of the staff. Some appeared shocked; they'd never met a chief of staff. Others expressed delight at having the ear of someone who was willing to listen. Much of that type of exchange went back to the secretary of state in the form of informational feedback. As the boss, he deserved to know what people in the department thought and how they felt.

Friends will tell you what you already know; strangers will tell you things you otherwise wouldn't know. Engage strangers in conversation. Ask who they are. Ask what they do. Ask how they do it. Even ask how they like what they do. The answers might surprise you.

Visit the product manufacturing or assembly line. Watch people and things in motion. Check their movements, watch their expressions, observe what they say and do on breaks. Introduce yourself and enter into a conversation with these important employees.

By going to the watercooler, you can meet new people. You can listen in on what people are saying. Much of the time it's about balls—footballs, basketballs, or baseballs, depending on the season. Other times, it's about what they do, who they do it for, and whether they enjoy the experience.

Whatever you learn, it is likely to be something to share with the boss, good or bad. He or she should want to know what's happening elsewhere in the company; the boss may even ask what you learned. Your bosses can use what you say as a barometer to measure what's going on out there that they don't normally see for themselves in the workplace.

By frequenting the various places and by engaging people in conversation, not only will you learn what's happening at that moment, you're likely to establish a contact or foster a relationship that can continue over time. Those new friends and acquaintances can become repeat sources of information, good or bad. If they come to know and trust you, those people will even confide in you things that they know but that you'd probably never know without them.

Who knows? A mentoring relationship might even develop. By virtue of your position, which is close to the boss, certainly closer than those of the persons with whom you're talking, they may feel you are perfectly positioned to hear them out or help them out.

Although traditional long-term mentoring relationships should be part of what you do as a leader over time with people who come to rely on you, situational mentoring is important too. Connecting with people with whom you come into contact momentarily or situationally allows you to interact for a certain period that may be as short as the lunch hour or longer when you see them the next time or over the course of time.

By virtue of this unempirical type of research, if you become aware of a problem and are in a position of responsibility, try to fix it yourself. If it's too big or too hot to handle, take it up the line. If you are high enough up that chain, you may be the one who takes the problem directly to the boss.

If you are ever the one who conveys bad tidings to the boss, come armed with a proposed solution. No boss wants to hear that something is wrong without hearing how to fix it.

Literally, the definition of *conscience* is "the faculty of recognizing the difference between right and wrong." This implies that you should be acting accordingly to do something about the matter one way or another. For any organization and for any boss, that is a valuable capability to have. For people in positions of responsibility, that is an important and crucial role to fulfill.

48

Bullying Is Bad for Business

Business schools and leadership coaches say the same thing: an autocratic bully or a corporate clown is bad for business. Whether it's about the bottom line or the use of a motivational technique, when people at the corporate table shove their ideas down the throats of others, it doesn't make for progress or good business.

As on an athletic team filled with talent, records can be broken as a result of striving for team outcome over individual credit. We all want to shine, to be seen as smart and important, but the force of style and personality can be dominant.

The boss can be an autocratic leader and browbeat the staff to achieve results. There are plenty of narcissists sitting at the head of team tables. Or you can encounter a high climber who has a next best idea every time you sit at that table. Either case is dysfunctional.

I once knew of a chief executive who would call subordinates to report to him on matters of importance. If he didn't get or hear what he wanted or expected, his technique for capturing the unwary staff officers' attention was to pick up a book and throw it at them. Some leaders have a penchant for beating up on the little guy.

Workplace bullying often involves an abuse or misuse of power. Typically, it creates in the abused feelings of defensiveness, and it undermines a person's right to his or her dignity at work.

Another form of bullying involves employees who individually bully their peers or even a group of coworkers targeting another worker. Regrettably, psychological aggression in the workplace is more common than it should be. By all rights this should not be allowed to be done anywhere or to anyone.

Forms of aggression by a manager toward a subordinate can range from unwarranted criticism to blame, exclusion, being yelled at, especially in the presence of others, or even excessive micromanaging. When it becomes entrenched in the culture of an organization, it simply becomes accepted as part of organizational behavior. Not good!

This happened to me when my office phone rang early one morning and the person on the line summoned me to the third-floor office of his boss, a rather important three-star general in the Pentagon. I suspected the cause immediately. A front-page *Washington Post* story that unforgettable day had suggested that the size of the U.S. Army, from that time in the mid-1980s going into the next decade and beyond, could actually grow far smaller as a result of new tactics and technology, such as the use of robots in place of soldiers.

Shudder at the thought, believed this general, especially since the notion of a probable downsizing was the departing forecast of the outgoing under secretary of the army, James Ambrose, a view the general strongly opposed.

As I entered the outer office of the deputy chief of staff for operations at the time, I was told by his executive assistant that I was to be seated—an intended purgatory. After the requisite 10-minute wait, I entered the general's impressively large office and felt uncomfortably small standing in front of his desk at rigid attention. After a second attention-grabbing wait as the general studied a document he'd no doubt put by design on his desk, he looked up and glared into my eyes. He picked up the *Washington Post* front section, pointed to the article on page 1, and asked in a gruff voice, "Are you responsible for this?"

"Well, yes, sir, in a manner of speaking. I arranged the interview for Mr. Ambrose," I told him. Actually, if the truth be known, when the under secretary told the late senior defense correspondent George Wilson his view of the future, I blanched and fidgeted, knowing we were going to be at the top of the news the next day.

Mr. Ambrose sensed my antacid moment, turned to me, and asked, "Something wrong?" Since it was an on-the-record interview and this would certainly go viral, I responded, "No, sir, as long as that's what you meant to say." He said that he stood behind his views that R&D would dominate and determine the army's future end strength.

At my inquisition the next day, the general was unimpressed with my explanation. He railed on about how it was wrong for civilian leaders to judge and predict what was right for his army. So much for civilian control of the military in a democratic society, I thought.

For me, it reinforced my long-held view that you can learn as much if not more from something gone wrong than you can when things go right. I left the general's office committed to the belief that displaced aggression is a fact of life but an anger-directed method I would continue to avoid at all costs.

I've seen similar bullying approaches by staff officers who are too smart or egotistical for their own good. It's as if they feel it's obligatory to dazzle their colleagues with their brilliance. They forever attempt to impress those present with their assertive view of things in the form of ideas they showcase as impressive even if they don't have to implement their bold initiatives.

Fortunately, I have been in a position to temper or tamp down those next best ideas without killing the instinct of the staff to think strategically. Chiefs of staff need to conduct the orchestra harmoniously before the sounds become a cacophony.

That is more art than science. Find a way to recognize the effort of developing an idea but also find a way to put that next best idea back in its box without embarrassing the inventor or discouraging the notion of thinking futuristically and innovatively.

When you have a lot of strong-minded people in a room, all of whom sound and act like pachyderms, you need to quiet the jungle. Building consensus is the key.

As chairman, Colin Powell was incredibly adept at doing this when he sat at the table with other members of the Joint Chiefs. After the fall of the former Soviet Union, the decision was made to downsize the armed forces. The Cold War was over, and, albeit for a different reason, Mr. Ambrose would have taken comfort in this call for fewer soldiers.

Each service chief—army, navy, and air force—wanted his share of the reduced pie. Loud sounds came from Powell's office during these Joint Chiefs' meetings. Yet at the end of the day, each of them had to give up more than he wanted to. Powell was able to bring them to that point.

The boss is left with the burden of doing something with contrasting ideas or faulty invention. A staff in critical positions surrounding that boss can act as both catalyst and conduit without killing the mood or the moment. A defective but thankful response is useful. Politicians have it down to a science when they typically begin a rebuttal by saying, "With all due respect, . . ."

Bullying is not limited to playgrounds or schools anymore. It's everywhere, not least in the halls of Congress and in C-suites. Workplace bullying has become a despicable trend that can wreak havoc on an organization if it is not met head-on. One way to do that is to have a clearly stated and widely distributed code of conduct. If your company doesn't have one, tell the boss you need it. You'll be doing him or her a great service.

49

Have Fun Along the Way

There is no common definition of fun. Having fun means different things to different people. Some people can't have fun even
on vacation. How sad! Some people can't find fun at the office.
How true!

Americans tend to overwork, overworry, and overdo things. We
have longer workweeks and less vacation time than other societies
around the world. Maybe it's time to take stock of what we choose
to derive from our time in the workplace.

There is no magic formula for putting a smile on one's face or
feeling good about being at work each day. However, there are
ways to get the most out of what you do in life. It starts with attitude; it continues with positive activities; it can end with events
that are remarkable.

Sometimes it's the unexpected that can lead to the ultimate
experience. For me, such a happening occurred in the fall of
1988. I hadn't been Admiral Bill Crowe's special assistant very
long when the now late *TIME* magazine correspondent Bruce van
Voorst walked into my office suggesting I had a problem in that
I worked for the most powerful military man on the face of the
earth yet no one knew who he was, what he did, or what he stood
for. Momentarily amused, I asked if perhaps he'd like to help me
change that by interviewing the chairman for *TIME*. Bruce enthusiastically agreed that it was a splendid idea.

Without telling the chairman he was an unknown in some circles, I recommend that he agree to the interview. The admiral and Bruce met in late November. It was a Q&A format, and it went well. The article was published in the December 26 issue of *TIME*. Everyone was pleased.

One of the questions Bruce asked the admiral was, "How does the most powerful military man alive relax?" The admiral responded that he enjoyed spending time with his family and also liked watching television. Bruce asked what his favorite television show was. The admiral told him it was the popular comedy series *Cheers*.

Over the holidays, feeling very proud of myself, I wondered where else I could take this moment of positive public exposure. Returning to work in early January, I picked up the phone and called a colleague in Los Angeles to ask for the name and phone number of the executive producer of *Cheers*. He called me back with the name and number of James Burrows.

I worked up the courage to call Burrows. I introduced myself as special assistant to Admiral William J. Crowe, Jr., the eleventh chairman of the Joint Chiefs of Staff. "Who?" was his response. He had reinforced Bruce's point. I told Burrows that the admiral had mentioned his program in an interview in the latest issue of *TIME*. Moreover, I suggested that if he'd like to take advantage of that compliment by asking the chairman to make a cameo appearance on *Cheers*, I was confident he'd agree to it. "Consider him asked," Burrows said. We hung up, and I felt my heart beating exceptionally fast. What had I just done? How could I ever pull this off? An answer presented itself the next day.

As was his wont, the admiral would visit staff offices on a regular basis. The next day he popped into mine and asked what was going on. I seized the moment by telling him that I had had a most interesting chat with the executive producer of *Cheers* and that he had asked if the admiral would make a cameo appearance on his show. "What do you think of that idea?" asked the admiral. "I think it's brilliant," was my response. The admiral reflected on the offer, agreed to it, and departed. Whew!

Before he could change his mind, I picked up the phone and called Burrows back and told him we were coming to Los Angeles in late January and could film it then. However, I told him there were two conditions: the script had to be done tastefully, and I had to be allowed to review it in advance. He agreed to both requests. If I hadn't raised those conditions, it would have been irresponsible, even potentially reckless.

The admiral memorized his lines in the well-written script. He even changed a few to suit him better, and we were off to Hollywood. We filmed the episode titled "Hot Rocks." It aired on March 18, 1989. It was funny, it was humanizing, and it revealed who this powerful man was, what he stood for, and what his important role on behalf of the nation was. Most of all, it revealed the character of the man to millions who might not previously have known of him.

From that point on, whenever the admiral would speak in public, he would refer to his cameo appearance on *Cheers* by saying it was the most fun time he'd ever had in his four years as chairman. For me it was a heartwarming moment to see the boss having fun and at the same time being introduced to the American public in a memorable way.

I had experienced a magical moment of taking a chance and succeeding. Not everyone can experience these magical moments. Yet we can all work harder to squeeze the most out of life both personally and professionally. That might mean taking a chance on something risky. That might mean trying the unusual on for size. Don't fear doing this. Obviously, consider both the intended and the unintended consequences of everything you do. Having fun can result in either of those outcomes. When it does turn out well, life can be better in a memorable way.

50

Evaluate Everything You Do

In relative terms, your life is but a snapshot in time. As you go through life, it is filled with things you did, people you met, places you visited, all sorts of experiences good and bad. You owe it to yourself personally and professionally to gain insight and knowledge from what you've done and seen.

The problem is that in many cases people of responsibility tend to collect information or data but take little time to analyze what they have before them. That is often the case because we think we don't have the time, we don't take the time, or we simply don't care. What a shame.

We invest in research and develop plans as a result of the factfinding we have done. We even communicate what we intend to do to implement those plans. We tend to get so busy moving on to the next event that we don't take the time to assess what we are doing or how we have done it. Therefore, it is no surprise that we don't always get things right.

I find that the evaluation process may be the most important step of all in the things we do. Gathering information about what we're doing and how we are doing it can lead to an analysis of that material that in turn can improve a product, a service, a program, or even a good name.

Although the responsibility for evaluations falls to program managers, we all should be in the hunt to determine how we are doing. Monitoring what you are doing or have done is the data collection phase. Evaluating that data is the analysis phase. Quality improvement is the desired outcome phase.

I grew up in the military, an institution that evaluates everything. It starts in basic training, when soldiers' living spaces and equipment are inspected daily. There are also weekly, monthly, and annual inspections of nearly everyone and everything. Why? First of all, to get it right. Second of all, to teach service members that if they fail, they are accountable. Thus, you prepare for every evaluation in a way that does not allow for failure. The evaluation process is ingrained in people.

Running an executive-level training program has obvious challenges. I know because I've run one. The expectations of the senior leaders attending are high, as are the expectations of the distinguished guest speakers who come before them in the classroom. Putting these senior leaders in the classroom is the easy part. Keeping them interested, focused, and satisfied is much harder.

Getting it right is something I have worked hard at by evaluating course components in a variety of ways as the director and program manager. Everything from a weekly written evaluation of subjects and speakers to soliciting verbal feedback at any time. Simple things such as the temperature of the room, whether the last speaker hit the mark, the quality of the meals we are providing at the hotel, and the pace of instruction. Such feedback is critical not just at the end of the course of instruction but at every point along the way so that adjustments can be made as necessary. Criticism is welcome, changes are made, and satisfaction is guaranteed.

As an advisor to a number of senior officials over the course of my career, I evaluated everything they said or did. Some of it I kept to myself to offer improvements the next time or over time. Often I provided feedback as soon as the event was over: everything from how they did to how it could have been done better. That takes a bit of courage if the feedback isn't positive, but any boss who's worth his or her salt will appreciate honest advice on how to do it better.

Self-evaluation is the same. If I have an assistant with me when I give a speech or a class, the first question I ask when I'm done is, "How did I do?" I want the answer to be honest, good or bad. More often than not, an assistant can do a better job than I can at reading the body language of audience attendees, sensing their attentiveness or lack of attentiveness, and even evaluating the quality of their questions as I concentrate on the answers. Another true gauge is the comments overheard after the talk. The goal is to raise the bar, to get it right, to make it better the next time.

Managers can and should conduct internal evaluations about everything for which they have responsibility. They should also seek it from stakeholders. Those stakeholders can range from a board of directors to the general public and from suppliers to customers. Online surveys, Internet chat rooms, telephone inquiries, and personal conversations are all helpful. Feedback is critical; information is invaluable. Improvements are essential and must be carried out.

One form of evaluation that many dread is the personal performance appraisal. Whether you are the one who writes the evaluation or the one who is being evaluated, it's not always fun, but it surely is important. How can improvements be made if we don't know what we are doing wrong? How can standards be met if we don't know how we are falling short?

Perhaps the most important evaluation of all is the personal, face-to-face kind. It is the one feared the most yet the one needed the most. If you are the writer of a personal evaluation, it needs to be an honest assessment. If you are the recipient, you need to accept that not everyone gets the top grade. But whatever block you are in, whatever supporting detail is written, it needs to be discussed in person with you as the individual in question.

As the evaluator, judge everything from the critical to the mundane. Seek input and provide feedback. The way a person spends his or her time, for example, is critically important. Tell that person how and why it needs to be done more productively if such is the case. If the way a person is behaving with coworkers needs to be improved, tell the person what adjustments he or she needs to make. If something as simple as a person's telephone etiquette isn't helpful to the company, tell that person how to do it differently.

If you are the supervisor, don't wait until the next evaluation to tell an employee how he or she has improved or not. Reinforcement of right and correction of wrong constitute important feedback. There is great relevance to these performance ratings, which can determine raises, bonuses, promotions, and benefits for those involved.

Whatever you evaluate, whenever you conduct the evaluation, you can store it or you can share it. I vote for sharing it and in most cases sharing it at least in general terms with the boss. That person wants it, needs it, and deserves it. Good or bad, that person has a right to know the health of the organization. As President Ronald Reagan advised in his farewell address to the nation in 1988, "Don't be afraid to see what you see."

Think of an evaluation as preventive medicine. Like an annual physical when the doctor prescribes something stronger than an aspirin because he or she finds the patient suffering from a malady, the evaluation can serve as an antibiotic. If the prognosis is good, the boss needs to know that, too. Positive feedback can lead to decisions that reinforce what is being done well.

The boss is the ultimate decision maker, and you are the provider of the information that allows him or her to do that job best. The boss's success as a leader and a manager depends on how he or she builds, educates, coaches, and evaluates his or her people. You can and should help the boss as a conscience who honestly and objectively evaluates all that you hear and see in your workplace world. It is your duty.

Acknowledgments

Good fortune has provided me with ample opportunities to experience deeds—both good and bad—from which to learn and grow. In my career I have been exposed to extraordinary people: some heroes, others examples of what not to be or do. But each offered lessons of life that are worth sharing.

This book is part of my "season of giving back." It allows me to offer to those seeking the lampposts and street signs on the highway of life some direction that can take them to successful and rewarding destinations.

To those who taught me how to navigate that road, thank you for sharing. For those wanting to learn, thank you for caring. May there be gratitude expressed and lessons shared herein.

With the encouragement of many to fill these pages, courtesy of McGraw-Hill, with nuggets mined over time, I trust you won't be disappointed. To those who stood by me in ways they know or may never know, I am deeply grateful for what you gave me and what you are to me. A special thanks for your belief in me. To you I dedicate this labor of love.

Index

About the Author

F. William Smullen was appointed as the director of national security studies at the Maxwell School of Citizenship and Public Affairs in June 2003. He is also Maxwell's Senior Fellow in National Security and a member of the faculty of Syracuse University's S.I. Newhouse School of Public Communications as a Professor of Public Relations.

Before his appointment at Syracuse University, he was the chief of staff to Secretary of State Colin L. Powell and of the U.S. Department of State beginning in January 2001. As principal advisor to the secretary, he was responsible for monitoring and evaluating the formulation and implementation of departmental policies. He was also involved in the planning and development of concept strategy associated with foreign policy matters.

A professional soldier for 30 years, he retired from the U.S. Army in 1993. His military career included a series of infantry and command and staff assignments at the platoon, company, battalion, brigade, and division levels, as well as several public affairs positions, including Media Relations Officer at West Point and Chief of Media Relations for the Department of the Army. Overseas army tours took him to Korea, to Panama, and twice to Vietnam. His military schooling included the army's Command and General Staff College and the Army War College. His military citations include the Defense Superior Service Medal, the Legion of Merit, the Bronze Star Medal, the Army Meritorious Service Medal, the Air Medal, the Combat Infantryman's Badge, and the Parachutist's Badge.

His last assignment on active duty was as special assistant to the eleventh and twelfth chairmen of the Joint Chiefs of Staff, Admiral William J. Crowe, Jr., and General Colin L. Powell. Upon leaving active duty, he became the executive assistant to General Powell, assisting with the writing and promotion of Powell's bestselling autobiography, *My American Journey*, published in 1995. From 1993 to 2001 he had daily responsibility for managing the general's private office and professional activities. Beginning in 1997, he doubled his responsibilities by becoming the chief of staff for America's Promise—The Alliance for Youth, which Powell chaired from May 1997 to January 2001.

Among his career accomplishments, he was elected to Syracuse University's S.I. Newhouse School of Public Communications Hall of Fame and the University of Maine ROTC Hall of Fame and he was chosen as the recipient of the University of Maine 2007 Alumni Career Award, which is the highest honor presented by the University of Maine Alumni Association. He received the 2007 Public Relations Society of America's Lloyd B. Dennis Distinguished Leadership Award.

He earned a bachelor of arts degree in business and economics from the University of Maine in 1962 and a master of arts degree in public relations from the S.I. Newhouse School of Public Communications at Syracuse University in 1974.

An accomplished speaker, he appears before audiences nationwide on subjects of contemporary and topical interest. Featured topics include those from his book *Ways and Means for Managing Up*.